50 Literacy Strategies for Beginning Teachers, 1–8

Second Edition

TERRY NORTON
Winthrop University

BETTY LOU JACKSON LAND
Winthrop University

PEARSON
Merrill
Prentice Hall

Upper Saddle River, New Jersey
Columbus, Ohio

Library of Congress Cataloging-in-Publication Data

Norton, Terry L.

  50 literacy strategies for beginning teachers, 1–8 / Terry L. Norton, Betty Lou Jackson Land. — 2nd ed.

    p. cm.

  Includes bibliographical references.

  ISBN 978-0-13-224302-5 (alk. paper)

1. Language arts (Elementary) 2. First year teachers—Handbooks, manuals, etc. I. Land, Betty Lou Jackson. II. Title. III. Title: Fifty literacy strategies resources for beginning teachers, 1–8.

  LB1576.N845 2008

  372.6'044—dc22
                                    2007005038

Vice President and Executive Publisher: Jeffery W. Johnson
Senior Editor: Linda Ashe Bishop
Senior Production Editor: Mary M. Irvin
Senior Editorial Assistant: Laura Weaver
Design Coordinator: Diane C. Lorenzo
Project Coordination: Andrew Jones, Carlisle Publishing Services
Cover Designer: Candace Rowley
Cover Image: Images.com
Production Manager: Pamela D. Bennett
Director of Marketing: David Gesell
Marketing Manager: Darcy Betts Prybella
Marketing Coordinator: Brian Mounts

This book was set in Times by Carlisle Publishing Services. It was printed and bound by Bind-Rite Graphics Company. The cover was printed by Phoenix Color Corp.

Pearson Prentice Hall™ is a trademark of Pearson Education, Inc.
Pearson® is a registered trademark of Pearson plc
Prentice Hall® is a registered trademark of Pearson Education, Inc.
Merrill® is a registered trademark of Pearson Education, Inc.

Pearson Education Ltd.
Pearson Education Singapore Pte. Ltd.
Pearson Education Canada, Ltd.
Pearson Education—Japan

Pearson Education Australia Pty. Limited
Pearson Education North Asia Ltd.
Pearson Educación de Mexico, S.A. de C.V.
Pearson Education Malaysia Pte. Ltd.

10 9 8 7 6 5 4 3 2 1
ISBN 13: 978-0-13-224302-5
ISBN 10:   0-13-224302-4

Preface

Background and Core Beliefs about Literacy

Welcome to the second edition of *50 Literacy Strategies for Beginning Teachers, 1–8*. In this edition we have revised and clarified some of the strategies in the earlier edition, updated and expanded the bibliographies on further reading, and identified strategies useful for English learners on the matrix that appears on the inside cover of this text. The major change, however, is the addition of 11 new strategies, particularly in the areas of word recognition and writing.

Like the first edition, this text represents our shared thinking about effective techniques for developing student competence in literacy and is based on our combined experience as educators in the field of language arts. As with the first edition, we also have maintained our core assumptions about literacy learning and teaching. These assumptions are based on research and best practice in literacy instruction. We have found that these beliefs work especially well with the diverse children we serve in the Learning Improvement Center at Winthrop University, where we teach both preservice and inservice candidates in teacher education.

Our Core Assumptions

Among our core beliefs underlying the strategies in this book are the following:

- students actively seek to construct meaning as they grow in literacy;
- literacy develops over time and includes each of the language arts of reading, writing, listening, speaking, viewing, and visually representing, all of which are interrelated and mutually support one another;
- classroom growth in literacy occurs best where language is not fragmented and otherwise used for inauthentic purposes;
- literacy development improves when language is used in functional settings with authentic *literature*—that is, literacy competencies are best fostered through real literature for real purposes;
- teachers contribute to student acquisition of literacy through direct instruction and scaffolding of learning, which includes activating and building background knowledge, modeling, guided practice, and eventual independent practice, all of which lead students to increasing independence as learners who take ownership for their accomplishments.

Organization and Special Features

Lesson plans may follow many formats. In this book, we suggest an instructional framework that divides literacy lessons into three basic parts: what happens *before* students read or are read to, what happens *during* reading, and what happens *after* reading. Potential users will find ideas to create direct instruction and scaffolding for learners through building or activating background as preparation for learning, through providing assistance during learning, and through elaboration and application as extensions of learning. Using this instructional framework for literacy lessons, students are viewed as active participants in the construction of meaning.

New and experienced teachers, literacy tutors in clinical settings, paraprofessionals, and parents who provide home-schooling will find that the strategies described should be used for learners once they have been assessed and need particular interventions to bolster strengths or to overcome needs in literacy. The examples of authentic literature that illustrate each strategy—whether for word recognition, vocabulary development, reading comprehension, or writing—serve as instances of how to teach literacy competencies in a meaningful context. Thus, we encourage teachers to adapt each strategy for the strengths and needs of their students and to use each strategy with literature that their students are currently engaged in.

As those who use this book examine ways to incorporate each of the strategies into their teaching, we suggest that they give explicit explanation to students on *what* strategy is being used as an aid to literacy growth; *why* it is helpful as a literacy technique; *how* it works; and *when* learners can use it in either a classroom or independent setting.

Although we could have organized the strategies in a number of ways, we decided to categorize them using literacy competency areas including word recognition, vocabulary development, comprehension, and writing. Because language arts are interrelated, however, many of the strategies can fit multiple areas, including strategies helpful for English learners. Hence, we have provided a matrix with each strategy to help identify these. (See inside Cover.)

Acknowledgments

We wish to thank the reviewers of our manuscript for their comments and insights: Timothy Shanahan, University of Illinois at Chicago; and Linda J. Button, University of Northern Colorado; Mark Esch, Arizona State University; and Brenda H. Spencer, California State University, Fullerton.

In addition, we want to thank the many gifted preservice and inservice teachers we have taught in courses at Winthrop University. Their implementations of the strategies included in this book have aided us immeasurably in producing this book, fine tuning each strategy, and ensuring its utility with students. We also wish to thank our students and graduate assistants Elizabeth Hall Eppes, Sara Carey Howard, and Jamie Kyzer and Stephanie Stancil for their technical assistance. We dedicate this book to the children who will benefit from its use.

Terry Norton
Professor of Reading

Betty Lou Jackson Land
Professor of Reading

Contents

PART I

Creating Successful Literacy Lessons

Format for Literacy Lessons

Effective literacy lessons have a similar underlying structure, no matter what the content of the lesson, whether the subject is dogs and cats or birds and bats. The same holds true for the literacy focus area of the lesson, whether it is deriving the meaning of a word from context or understanding story grammar through story mapping. This underlying structure also applies to lessons on narrative or expository text, no matter what the grade level of learners, whether kindergarten or beyond. The framework upon which a literacy plan is built has three core components that follow a specific instructional sequence of activities that occur *before* reading, *during* reading, and *after* reading.

In the *before,* or prereading, stage the teacher establishes for students a purpose for learning by describing what the topic of the lesson is and why it is important. Concurrent with the discussion of purpose is an activation of schema, or prior knowledge, that learners possess concerning the topic. If the teacher discovers that students have little or no prior knowledge, then background experiences must be established and related to the content of the lesson. Besides activating current background or implanting new knowledge, the prereading stage involves motivating reader interest in the topic. Thus, before reading occurs, both cognitive and affective domains of learning are crucial considerations of good literacy instruction that will prepare students for the *during* reading phase of a lesson.

During reading, students interact with text and bring to their learning the schema and interest aroused *before* reading. The teacher's role is to prompt active responses to reading by encouraging students to talk, write, think, or be creative as they construct meaning from text. Much of what students comprehend at this stage of a literacy lesson will derive from the success of the preparatory activities that came *before* reading.

After reading is a follow-up stage. At this point in the instructional framework, the teacher and students extend ideas from the lesson by elaborating further upon them, applying the ideas in different contexts, or making connections to other reading and life experiences. In short, postreading is a time of enrichment for learners.

Along with the aforementioned three-stage instructional framework, effective literacy lessons should be embedded with a universal teaching strategy composed of several steps. These may vary as to whether they occur *before, during,* or *after* reading and as to the particular emphasis allotted to each. Procedures for this generalizable teaching strategy follow.

Procedures for Generalizable Teaching Strategy

The generalizable teaching strategy contained within the instructional framework of literacy lessons has six steps. These should be part of any specific strategy the teacher uses to foster growth in literacy competencies such as word recognition, vocabulary, comprehension, and writing. For example, if the teacher is developing student facility with story grammar elements like setting, characters, problem, problem-resolution attempts, resolution, and theme, a specific strategy that might aid student understanding of these components is a story pyramid or a variation thereon. (See pages 91–94.) As use of the story pyramid unfolds throughout the literacy lesson, we suggest its deployment should be explicitly related to students in terms of the following six steps of the generalizable teaching strategy.

Step 1:   Explain WHAT

The teacher should explain *what* a story pyramid is. This would normally occur *before* reading as part of building background, this time for a specific strategy, not just for a specific content.

Step 2:   Ask WHY

The teacher should explain *why* a story pyramid is helpful in developing an understanding of story grammar. This step, too, would likely occur *before* reading as part of the motivation for learning.

Step 3:   Ask WHEN

As a further part of *before* reading, the teacher should indicate to students *when* to use a story pyramid—that is, when one is trying to understand the organization of narrative text (i.e., stories). Again, this step probably is best suited for *before* reading.

Step 4:   MODEL how

At this point, the teacher may also wish to engage in the fourth step of the generalizable teaching strategy—*modeling how* to do a story pyramid with something students have already completed reading, further activating prior knowledge and relating it to new learning. Thus, *modeling how* to complete in part or in whole a story pyramid may be done *before* reading. However, *modeling* might occur *during* or *after* reading as students answer questions and react to the literature they are presently studying.

Step 5:   Require GUIDED PRACTICE

When students engage in unfamiliar strategies to achieve growth in literacy, they need guided practice. For instance, in completing a story pyramid for the first time, learners will profit by having the teacher direct their work through positive reinforcement of correct answers and corrective feedback on incorrect or incomplete ones. Guided practice requires the teacher to serve as a mentor, helping students work through interactions with text as they move toward independence in learning. This step may take place *during* or *after* reading in the instructional sequence.

Step 6:   Provide opportunities for INDEPENDENT PRACTICE

Independent practice is the final step of the generalizable teaching strategy. In the case of a story pyramid, students complete the pyramid as they map the organization of narrative selection by themselves. They are on their own in the *after* reading phase of a literacy lesson.

When teachers plan and deliver instruction, they often focus exclusively on steps 1 and 6 of the generalizable teaching strategy. For example, in teaching a literature selection in which they use a specific strategy like a story pyramid, they may tell students what a story pyramid is and then expect them to complete one as part of a postreading check for comprehension. However, short-circuiting instruction in this way may lead to frustration on the part of learners. Steps 2 through 5 are essential components of creating success in literacy development.

The story pyramid is only one of numerous specific literacy strategies available to teachers, many of them described in detail in the different sections of this book. Nonetheless, the procedures given here for the generalizable teaching strategy should be used concurrently with any specific strategy selected for a learner's needs in a literacy lesson. (See Figure I–1.)

Teacher's Name: *Miss Ginger Lark*
Grade Level: *Grade Three*
Literacy Area of Focus: *Story grammar elements including character, setting, problem-resolution, and theme*
Assessment Source: *Informal reading inventory with narrative retelling; teacher observation*
Literature Used: *Arthur's Teacher Trouble,* by Marc Brown

ACTIVITIES	TEACHING PROCEDURES (before, during and after reading)	TEACHER REFLECTIONS (How did the lesson go?)
Before Reading		
• Introduce purpose statement for students. • Activate prior knowledge or build background knowledge. • Engage learner interest • Create a story web chart.	• To activate prior knowledge, ask questions: "How did you feel about your teacher on the first day of school? Did you think he or she was mean? What did you think after you were in class for a while? What do teachers do when students do not listen? Would you think a teacher was mean if he got angry with his students for not listening?" • Say: "We will be reading a story about a teacher that everyone thinks is the meanest teacher in school. As we read this story, we will be looking for specific information such as the names of the story characters, where the story takes place, and events that happen in the story. As we learn about this information, we will put it in a chart that organizes the information to help us remember what we have read." • "Let's begin by taking a picture walk through our story, *Arthur's Teacher Trouble,* by Marc Brown. I will point out characters and locations in the story during our picture walk. I would like you to predict what you think will happen when we read the story."	

FIGURE I–1 Example of a Successful Literacy Lesson Plan

3

During Reading	
• Engage students in shared reading: reading *aloud,* reading *along,* reading *alone.* • Discuss story elements to complete the story web.	• Ensure all students have a copy of *Arthur's Teacher Trouble.* Then, start by reading the beginning of the book *aloud* including the part that tells about the spelling contest and that introduces Arthur's teacher, Mr. Ratburn. Check to see that students are following along in their books. • After a while, ask students to orally read *along* with you the part of the story that tells about the class studying for the spelling contest. • Then, ask students to finish the book *alone,* reading silently the part of the story that tells about the spelling contest. • During the reading *aloud,* reading *along,* and reading *alone,* stop to ask students to respond to the characters' actions by discussing what Arthur learned or how he changed. Guide the questioning to help students derive an understanding of the theme of the story and the central problem or key conflict.
After Reading	
• Model how to complete a story web that includes characters, setting, problem-resolution, and theme. • Engage students in guided practice, prompting them to find the story elements. • Provide independent practice, prompting if needed, to help students complete a new story web for a different story. • Use the story web chart for an extension activity for writing a summary of the original story.	• Introduce the story web chart. (See Figure I–2.) Say: "This is a web that will help you think about different parts of the story. It is shaped like a spider web because parts of the story branch out from the central idea of the story. In this web, you will see that to help us understand the elements of a story, we need to find the names of the main characters, the story setting, the problem the story tells about, and the solution or resolution for that problem. It will also help us think about the theme or main idea of the story."

FIGURE I–1   *Continued*

- Beginning with the bubble for main character, model how to fill in the story web chart. "The name of our story today is *Arthur's Teacher Trouble,* by Marc Brown, so I will write that in the center of the web. Although there were other characters, the main character is Arthur, so I will fill his name in the circle called 'Main Character.' Are there any other names I should put in this circle?"
- If needed, complete the whole chart together as a class as a part of the modeling process. If students understand how to complete the chart, provide them with guided practice time to fill it in. Scaffold instruction in order to work with small groups of students who need more direction.
- For independent practice, ask students to read a new story and try completing a story web chart for it.

FIGURE I–1 *Continued*

Purpose: To discuss and summarize story grammar elements of setting, main characters, problem, resolution, and theme.

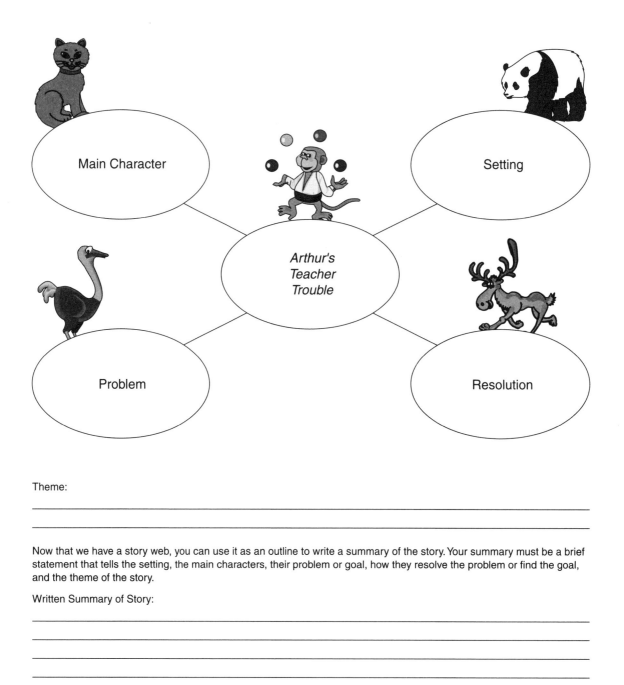

Theme:
_____
_____

Now that we have a story web, you can use it as an outline to write a summary of the story. Your summary must be a brief statement that tells the setting, the main characters, their problem or goal, how they resolve the problem or find the goal, and the theme of the story.

Written Summary of Story:
_____
_____
_____
_____

FIGURE I–2   Story Web Chart

FURTHER READING

Taylor, B., Harris, L. A., Pearson, P. D., & Garcia, G. (1995). *Reading difficulties: Instruction and assessment* (2nd ed.). New York: McGraw-Hill.

Tompkins, G. E. (2005). *Language arts: Patterns of Practice* (6th ed.) Upper Saddle River, NJ: Merrill/Prentice Hall.

Tierney, R. J., & Readence, J. E. (2000). *Reading strategies and practices: A compendium* (5th ed.). Boston: Allyn & Bacon.

PART II

Word Recognition Strategies: Sight Words, Context Clues, Morphemic (Structural) Analysis, and Phonic Analysis

Pocket Chart

Strategy at a Glance: *Grade Levels 1–3*

When to Use	Grouping	Literature Type	Skill Areas
● before reading	● individual	● narrative	● word recognition
○ during reading	● small group	● expository	● vocabulary
● after reading	● whole class		● comprehension
	● center		● writing

Purpose

To develop the ability to construct meaning after a story has been read and to increase sight vocabulary for pronouncing words automatically for reading fluency

Literature Used

Free Fall, by David Wiesner

When to Use

Before and after reading

Description of Strategy

Pocket charts are large, heavy paper, cloth, or plastic charts that have pockets where words or sentences may be placed. Words from a story or poem may be printed on strips or on word cards of the same size. A teacher might also use words from student dictation. The teacher can then use the word cards from the selected literature for a number of different activities.

Procedures for Use

1. Since a wordless picture book was chosen for this strategy, students will create a story to go with the illustrations. The teacher and students will first interact with the book and each other through discussion and questioning about the storyline revealed through the pictures. The teacher then records the students' partial or full retelling of the story one sentence at a time on sentence strips. It will be helpful as reinforcement of sight words for learners to watch as the teacher records and recites their rendition.

The length of the story will depend on the students and the book. Less able learners may tell a story about only one picture from a wordless book, while those who are more capable may create a narrative for all of the illustrations. Retellings of longer texts may need to occur over several lessons.

2. The teacher reads the story *aloud*; then the teacher and students orally read the story *along* together; and finally the students read the story *aloud* and *alone*. (This technique is referred to as read *aloud, along, alone*.)

> The boy is dreaming.

> He goes places in his dream.

3. The teacher now uses the sentence strips and writes each word of the retold story on a separate card. The cards should be the same size and written in the style of letters students are accustomed to reading. They should watch the teacher record the words and should pronounce them with the teacher.

| The | boy | is | dreaming. |

4. The teacher puts the words to the story in the pocket chart in order.

5. The teacher once again reads the retelling *aloud*; teacher and students then read the story *along together orally*; and finally students read the story *aloud* and *alone* as the teacher sweeps his or her fingers under the words on the pocket chart to help readers with the flow. (These repetitions will enhance the students' ability to read the story.)

6. The teacher now takes out two to three word cards that the students could not read from the pocket chart and places them on a table. The teacher also may get out a box of sand in which these students will write the word from the word card. (This method will reinforce these words as sight words for tactile learners.) The students write each word with a finger in the sand as the word is pronounced, a procedure that should be repeated for all word cards on the table that were removed from the pocket chart and that students could not read. It is best to select only a few (two to three) difficult words for such sight word practice. The visual image, or configuration, of the words selected should be different.

7. As an additional reinforcement activity, the teacher may next place all of the word cards from the pocket chart story on the table in a shuffled stack. From these, students place the word cards in the correct order in the pocket chart so that both the teacher and students can again read the story *aloud* in the correct sequence.

8. Students may read the story *aloud* and *alone* if further practice and reinforcement are needed.

FURTHER READING

Cooper, J. D. (2000). *Literacy: Helping children construct meaning* (4th ed.). Boston: Houghton Mifflin.

Cunningham, P. (2000). *Phonics they use* (3rd ed.). New York: Longman.

Cunningham, P., & Allington, R. (1994). *Classrooms that work*. New York: HarperCollins.

Reutzel, D. R., & Cooter, R. (2000). *Teaching children to read: Putting the pieces together* (3rd ed.). Columbus, OH: Merrill.

2

Word Wall for Sound-Symbol Relationships

(EL) *Also beneficial when working with English learners*

Strategy at a Glance: *Grade Levels 1–3*

When to Use	Grouping	Literature Type	Skill Areas
○ before reading	○ individual	● narrative	● word recognition
○ during reading	● small group	● expository	● vocabulary
● after reading	● whole class		○ comprehension
	○ center		○ writing

Purpose

To integrate writing and reading and to reinforce grapheme-phoneme (sound-symbol) relationships

Literature Used

The Dog That Called the Signals, by Matt Christopher

Teammates, by Peter Golenbock

When to Use

After reading

Description of Strategy

A word wall is an instructional tool that may build on the need to further develop word recognition skills. It may be used with students who need assistance with beginning or ending consonant sounds and medial long or short vowel sounds. The words may come from a book, topic of interest, or words the teacher knows that learners are having difficulty with. The words are placed on a poster or chart (i.e., the word wall) for students to see and refer to in further reading and writing activities. The words on the wall should follow a language pattern as with the initial consonant /f/ for *The Dog That Called the Signals* or with the short medial /a/ sound illustrated in *Teammates*.

Procedures for Use

1. With students, the teacher selects a book containing words that they need to work on and that have the same pattern, in this case the initial sound of /f/ in words in *The Dog That Called the Signals* or the short medial /a/ in *Teammates*.

2. With the teacher's assistance, students choose from the book words that follow the identified sound pattern, in this case /f/ or short /a/. A chart, picture, diagram, web, and so on may be used by the teacher as a place to write the words and hang them on the wall. (See examples for *The Dog That Called the Signals* and *Teammates* in Figures 2–1 and 2–2.) These should be written in the style that learners will encounter in print. The words may be written on cards and displayed on the word wall with tape, tacks, or Velcro. This way, the words are easily moved around for a variety of purposes.

3. For additional practice, the teacher works with students to select other words to illustrate the sound pattern. This activity will help students solidify their knowledge of the pattern as they make connections to their experiential background with words already familiar to them and not in their reading.

4. As the teacher does other kinds of literacy activities in the class, he or she may choose words from the word wall to use in lessons and in examples. These may include writing activities. For example, an extension of this strategy would be to take the words from the word wall and write a sentence using each one or to write a summary of the book or a whole story incorporating some or all of the words.

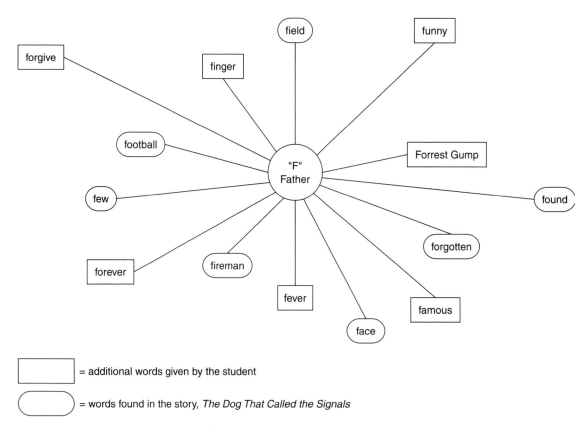

☐ = additional words given by the student

◯ = words found in the story, *The Dog That Called the Signals*

FIGURE 2–1   Example for Initial Consonant /f/ in *The Dog Called the Signals*
Note: Words that begin with a blend, such as "flower" and "friend," should not be used to illustrate initial /f/ when students are first learning the sound.

Beginning of the Book	Middle of the Book		End of the Book	
bl**a**ck	m**a**nager	(first syllable)	h**a**d	
b**a**ck	f**a**ns		c**a**n	
	br**a**nch		s**a**ddens	(first syllable)

FIGURE 2–2   Example for Medial Short /a/ in *Teammates*

FURTHER READING

Cunningham, P. (2000). *Phonics they use* (3rd ed.). New York: Longman.

Cunningham, P., & Allington, R. (1994). *Classrooms that work.* New York: HarperCollins.

Cunningham, P. M., Moore, S. A., Cunningham, J. W., & Moore, D. W. (1995). *Reading and writing in elementary classrooms: Strategies and observations* (3rd ed.). White Plains, NY: Longman.

Gunning, T. (2005). *Creating literacy instruction for all students* (5th ed.). Boston: Allyn & Bacon.

Johns, J., & Lenski, S. D. (2001). *Improving reading: Strategies and resources* (3rd ed.). Dubuque, IA: Kendall/Hunt.

Reutzel, D. R., & Cooter, R. (2000). *Teaching children to read: Putting the pieces together* (3rd ed.). Columbus, OH: Merrill.

Tompkins, G. E. (2005). *Language arts: Patterns of practice* (6th ed.). Upper Saddle River, NJ: Merrill/Prentice Hall.

Vacca, J. A. L., Vacca, R. T., & Gove, M. K. (2000). *Reading and learning to read* (4th ed.). New York: Addison Wesley Longman.

Modified Cloze Technique

EL *Also beneficial when working with English learners*

Strategy at a Glance: *Grade Levels All*

When to Use	Grouping	Literature Type	Skill Areas
● before reading	● individual	● narrative	● word recognition
● during reading	● small group	● expository	● vocabulary
● after reading	○ whole class		● comprehension
	○ center		○ writing

Purpose

To develop the ability to use context clues and grapheme-phoneme awareness (sound-symbol relationships) for pronunciation of words and construction of meaning

Literature Used

"The Man in the Moon As He Sails the Sky," an anonymous poem

When to Use

During or after reading

Description of Strategy

Cloze is an instructional tool that uses a blank space to show the deletion of words or word parts, such as letters, and that can readily be adapted to satisfy the needs of remedial readers. For those who need assistance with beginning, middle, or ending sounds (graphophonemic clues), a letter or letters may be provided as a prompt at the beginning, middle, or end of a blank. Students must then use additional clues (contextual) to determine what the missing word is. Because this strategy is a modified cloze approach, it is not necessary to have a fixed deletion pattern of every *n*th word, as is often the case when cloze is used for prereading assessment. The teacher simply deletes words with the beginning, middle, or ending sound that students need practice with, as in the example in step 4 of the following procedures. The blanks, however, should be of equal length so as not to provide extraneous typographical clues. Because the modified cloze technique requires learners to use context clues, it also works well as a vocabulary development strategy for deriving word meaning.

📎 Procedures for Use

1. The teacher selects a poem or story that has an interesting pattern and opportunities for using context clues to help pronounce words and construct meaning.

2. After the poem is selected, it is retyped in large print, and letter from the stimulus words are omitted, such as those containing medial short /i/ in the consonant-vowel-consonant pattern (CVC) in the poem, "The Man in the Moon As He Sails the Sky." (See lines 2–8 of the poem.)

3. Before students supply the missing words, they and the teacher discuss how to figure out what the missing words are. The teacher may model the process, or do a "think aloud," with one example and then encourage learners to reflect on the use of the surrounding words to determine the missing word for each of the other blanks.

4. The following poem builds both grapheme-phoneme awareness (in this case with short medial /i/) and contextual awareness. However, in this poem, the initial /m/ sound could be emphasized, if needed, in words like "Man," "Moon," "made," "mistake," "milk," and "milky," so that lines might read as "The M____ in the M____ as he sails the sky. . . ." Poetry is good to use because of the repetition of sounds with either assonance (for vowels) or alliteration (for consonants).

> The Man in the Moon as he sails the sky
> Is a very remarkable sk____pper,
> But he made a m____stake when he tried to take
> A drink of m____lk from the d____pper.
> He d____pped right out of the M____lky Way
> And slowly and carefully f____lled it.
> The B____g Bear growled and the L__ttle Bear howled,
> And frightened h____m so that he sp____lled it!

5. For further practice, students might discuss words like "is," "in," and "it" in the poem since these, too, illustrate short /i/ at the beginning of words.

FURTHER READING

Cunningham, P. (2000). *Phonics they use* (3rd ed.). New York: Longman.

Cunningham, P., & Allington, R. (1994). *Classrooms that work*. New York: HarperCollins.

Graves, M., Juel, C., & Graves, B. (1998). *Teaching reading in the 21st century*. Needham Heights, MA: Allyn & Bacon.

Harris, A. J., & Sipay, E. R. (1990). *How to increase reading ability: A guide to developmental and remedial methods* (9th ed.). New York: Longman.

Johns, J., & Lenski, S. D. (2001). *Improving reading: Strategies and resources* (3rd ed.). Dubuque, IA: Kendall/Hunt.

Reutzel, D. R., & Cooter, R. (2000). *Teaching children to read: Putting the pieces together* (3rd ed.). Columbus, OH: Merrill.

Tierney, R. J., & Readence, J. E. (2000). *Reading strategies and practices: A compendium* (5th ed.). Boston: Allyn & Bacon.

Masking

 Also beneficial when working with English learners

Strategy at a Glance: *Grade Levels 1–3*

When to Use	Grouping	Literature Type	Skill Areas
○ before reading	● individual	● narrative	● word recognition
○ during reading	● small group	● expository	● vocabulary
● after reading	○ whole class		○ comprehension
	○ center		○ writing

Purpose

To help students develop grapheme-phoneme (sound-symbol) awareness by focusing on word beginnings and endings that are familiar to them

Literature Used

The Blah, by Jack Kent

When to Use

After reading

Description of Strategy

Masking may be used to allow learners to focus on a single word sound, or a grapheme-phoneme component, in familiar sight words to extend automaticity to unknown words. Students will learn that by simply changing the initial or final letter(s), they can form new words. The technique, as described here, is thus helpful in improving the word recognition skill of phonics, which is most successful when students first develop a concept of a word and then relate it to the printed letters for sounds. Accordingly, the teacher should read the book first so that the students are able to hear each of the words used in context. The teacher should switch the initial and final phonemes—that is, whichever sounds are chosen for emphasis—of selected words to form new words.

⊗ Procedures for Use

1. The literature selected for this masking exercise is *The Blah*. It contains words with spelling patterns for rhyming words to develop sound-symbol relationships.

2. After the literature has been read in a shared mode such as *along* or *aloud*, the teacher selects several words the students know—for example, "sad" and "fish."

3. The first words selected should be words where the initial phoneme can be changed to make new words. Changing the initial phoneme develops rhyming words (that is, word families based on phonograms like –ad in "sad" or –ish in "fish"). It is easier for students to hear the beginning sound of the word rather than the final sound.

4. Masking slides and holders should be made prior to the activity. The teacher creates a masking slide by first deciding on the phonogram to be taught. The teacher can have every possible letter option for the phonogram written on the card for the masking activity or leave a couple of examples blank and let the students provide letters that could be substituted to form new words.

5. The following illustration is for "fish," a word from *The Blah*. The masking strip shows how a rhyming word family is created with "wish," "dish," and "swish." Of course, combinations of letters such as consonant blends and digraphs, as with "sw" for "swish," may be used instead of single letters to create the rhyming word family.

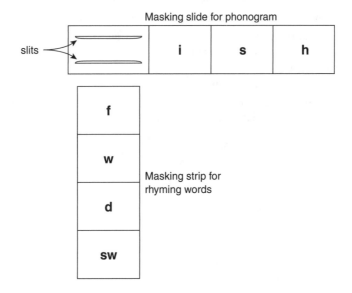

6. When students are able to use successfully the masking activity with initial letters or letter combinations, the teacher can begin working with masking activities to change the final sounds of words as in the following masking slide and strip:

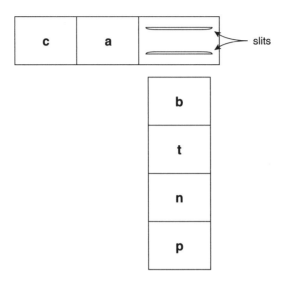

FURTHER READING

Cunningham, P. (2000). *Phonics they use* (3rd ed.). New York: Longman.

Cunningham, P., & Allington, R. (1994). *Classrooms that work.* New York: HarperCollins.

Graves, M., Juel, C., & Graves, B. (1998). *Teaching reading in the 21st century.* Needham Heights, MA: Allyn & Bacon.

Johns, J., & Lenski, S. D. (2001). *Improving reading: Strategies and resources* (3rd ed.). Dubuque, IA: Kendall/Hunt.

Reutzel, D. R., & Cooter, R. (2000). *Teaching children to read: Putting the pieces together* (3rd ed.). Columbus, OH: Merrill.

5

Language Experience Approach for Sight Word Development

$\widehat{EL}$ *Also beneficial when working with English learners*

Strategy at a Glance: *Grade Levels All*

When to Use	Grouping	Literature Type	Skill Areas
● before reading	● individual	● narrative	● word recognition
● during reading	● small group	● expository	● vocabulary
● after reading	● whole class		● comprehension
	○ center		● writing

Purpose

To improve reading by helping students develop a basic sight word vocabulary for automaticity

Literature Used

The Rainbow Fish, by Marcus Pfister

When to Use

Before, during, and after reading

Description of Strategy

In the language experience approach, students, individually or in groups, dictate a story as the teacher records it. The written story is based on the students' oral language and personal experience, whether built by the teacher or already possessed by the students. These features of language experience increase the likelihood that students, particularly low-achieving readers, will be able to read and comprehend the dictated text since the words are their own and not those of another writer, which may or may not correspond to the students' language. Student success with this approach provides a motivational boost for learners because they usually take pride in the experience stories created. Older, less able readers will often find that the stories are at an appropriate maturity level, unlike stories in beginning basals, which may be at an appropriate reading ability level but seem too immature in context. Although the language experience approach may be used to teach many aspects of literacy, such as sequencing, spelling, comprehension of expository or narrative grammar of texts, and so forth, the focus in the following procedures is on using language experience stories to develop a stock of basic sight words to promote automaticity in reading.

The teacher selects any topic important to the students. This serves as the basis for the dictated experience. Such a topic might be "my favorite place to visit," "my summer vacation," or "my favorite animal." If used for a group story, the experience might be about the class pet, a field trip, or another experience with which the class is familiar. In addition, literature can be used to build background and write a story summary. The literature might be a story in a basal reader, a passage from a content area textbook like science, or a children's book like *The Rainbow Fish*.

Procedures for Use

1. The teacher engages the student or group in a brief discussion about *The Rainbow Fish* in order to build background. A picture walk would be an appropriate strategy to incorporate at this stage. (See pages 91–92.)

2. The teacher reads the book *aloud*. During this step, guided listening questions that call for prediction or that help learners attend to significant concepts and details such as important vocabulary words or key elements of story grammar like setting, characters, sequence of events, and descriptive passages may help improve comprehension and later retelling.

3. Students may orally summarize the story or part of the story as the teacher records what is dictated. (In some instances, the dictation may be about an experience that is merely related to the literature or that is inspired by it, as in the following example in item 8 on *The Rainbow Fish*.) Whether chart paper, the chalkboard, or notebook paper is used to record the dictation, students should be able to see the words as the teacher reads them *aloud* in order to aid in establishing them as sight words. The teacher should be sure the words are those of the students themselves so that they feel ownership for the story. It is important to keep the dictation short at first. If the story is too long, less capable learners may not be able to read it.

4. When the dictation is completed, the teacher should read the dictated story *aloud* and point to each word as students follow *along*. This procedure further helps to build a sight word vocabulary for words that students already possess as part of a speaking vocabulary but have not yet learned in their written form. As the teacher reads the story, learners should be given an opportunity to make any changes.

5. Once changes are completed, the teacher and students read the story together, with the teacher again pointing with smooth motion at each word as it is read *along*.

6. Students now try reading the story *alone*. If there are any words at this point that they cannot pronounce, the teacher should note these for later practice and review. These might go into a personal word bank or word wall that may serve as individual dictionaries for future reference for reading or for writing stories.

7. When the teacher feels confident that students have mastered the words as sight words for the dictated story, a final activity could be to have the story rewritten as an additional summary and illustrated with a picture if students so desire.

8. Figure 5–1 shows an experience story, titled "The Colorful Fish," based on *The Rainbow Fish*. The words in the list are those with which further practice was needed by the children who dictated the story.

The Colorful Fish

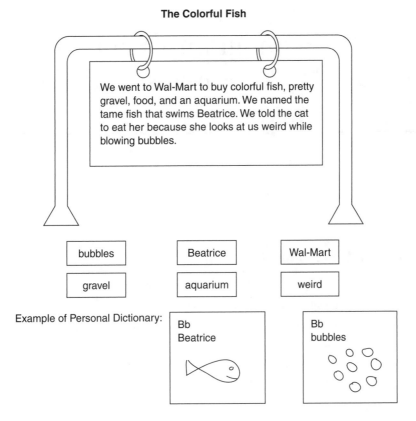

Example of Personal Dictionary:

FIGURE 5–1   The Colorful Fish

FURTHER READING

Cunningham, P. (2000). *Phonics they use* (3rd ed.). New York: Longman.

Cunningham, P., & Allington, R. (1994). *Classrooms that work*. New York: HarperCollins.

Cunningham, P. M., Moore, S. A., Cunningham, J. W., & Moore, D. W. (1995). *Reading and writing in elementary classrooms: Strategies and observations* (3rd ed.). White Plains, NY: Longman.

Graves, M., Juel, C., & Graves, B. (1998). *Teaching reading in the 21st century*. Needham Heights, MA: Allyn & Bacon.

Gunning, T. (2005). *Creating literacy instruction for all students* (5th ed.). Boston: Allyn & Bacon.

Norton, D. E., & Norton, S. E. (2003). *Through the eyes of a child: An introduction to children's literature* (6th ed.). Upper Saddle River, NJ: Merrill/Prentice Hall.

Reutzel, D. R., & Cooter, R. (2000). *Teaching children to read: Putting the pieces together* (3rd ed.). Columbus, OH: Merrill.

Taylor, B., Harris, L. A., Pearson, P. D., & Garcia, G. (1995). *Reading difficulties: Instruction and assessment* (2nd ed.). New York: McGraw-Hill.

Tierney, R. J., & Readence, J. E. (2000). *Reading strategies and practices: A compendium* (5th ed.). Boston: Allyn & Bacon.

Tompkins, G. E. (2005). *Language arts: Patterns of practice* (6th ed.). Upper Saddle River, NJ: Merrill/Prentice Hall.

6 Phonograms: Hink Pinks, Hinky Pinkies, and Hinkety Pinketies

Strategy at a Glance: *Grade Levels All*			
When to Use	**Grouping**	**Literature Type**	**Skill Areas**
○ before reading	● individual	● narrative	● word recognition
○ during reading	● small group	● expository	● vocabulary
● after reading	● whole class		○ comprehension
	○ center		● writing

Purpose

To reinforce word patterns or graphemic bases and develop spelling ability

Literature Used

Fish Is Fish, by Leo Lionni

When to Use

After reading

Description of Strategy

Hink pinks, hinky pinkies, or hinkety pinketies are pairs of rhyming words that are answers to riddles. The teacher gives the riddle, and the students respond with a pair of rhyming words.

Procedures for Use

1. *Before* reading, the teacher introduces the book *Fish Is Fish* to students by showing the cover and beginning a discussion about their experiences with fish. (A pet? A fishing trip to the river? Fish in tanks at the pet store?)

2. The teacher encourages students to listen to the story about two friends. One friend is a fish and one is a frog. The teacher explains that, after the story, she will ask the class to think of words that sound alike at the end such as "frog," "log," and "dog," or "fish," "wish," and "dish." The teacher reads the story while the class listens.

3. *During* reading, the teacher briefly pauses several times to get the students to orally name a word that rhymes with a word from the story. Examples may be "<u>weeds</u>" and "seeds"; "<u>bank</u>" and "tank"; "<u>jump</u>" and "bump." The underlined words are in the story.

4. *After* reading, the teacher explains that she is going to give some clues and the class will have to think of rhyming words to guess the riddle. For example, in the first clue below, "a dream or request made by a water animal," the answer would be a "fish wish." The rhyming words connect in their meaning to create a new word phrase. Some ideas are listed. (Underlined words are from the story.)

Clue	Hink Pinks
a dream or request made by a water animal from our story	<u>fish</u> - wish
an animal that is in the air, so it does not get wet	<u>dry</u> - butterfly
a big stick in the water with an animal on it trying to get warm	<u>frog</u> - log
water you can swim in that is not hot	<u>cool</u> - pool
a place to play—except at night	<u>dark</u> - park
a special time on the first date after the month of April	<u>May</u> - day

5. For those learners having difficulty guessing the answers to the riddles, the teacher can provide one of the words in the hink pink and the students can guess the rhyming word. "A <u>frog</u> sits on a big stick to get dry. This would be a <u>frog</u>-_____ ."

6. The teacher could begin with the riddles in this way to provide scaffolding. Gradually, she would give the clues as written and let the class guess both rhyming words. Eventually, boys and girls can create their own riddles with rhyming words as answers.

7. Pairs of words that are two-syllable answers to riddles are called hinky pinkies, while answers of three syllables are called hinkety pinketies.

Examples:

Hinky Pinkies	Hinkety Pinketies
a violent tale	stealing by thieves who think they are better than other people
<u>gory</u> - story	<u>robbery</u> - snobbery

FURTHER READING

Gipe, J. P. (2006). *Multiple paths to literacy: Assessment and differentiated instruction for diverse learners, K–12* (6th ed.). Upper Saddle River, NJ: Merrill/Prentice Hall.

Tompkins, G. E. (2005). *Language arts: Patterns of practice* (6th ed.). Upper Saddle River, NJ: Merrill/Prentice Hall.

7

Word Building

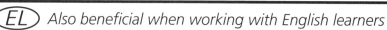 *Also beneficial when working with English learners*

Strategy at a Glance: *Grade Levels 1–2*			
When to Use	**Grouping**	**Literature Type**	**Skill Areas**
○ before reading	● individual	● narrative	● word recognition
○ during reading	● small group	● expository	○ vocabulary
● after reading	● whole class		○ comprehension
	○ center		○ writing

⸫ Purpose

To develop phonemic awareness or sound-symbol (phoneme-grapheme) correspondence and spelling

⸫ Literature Use

How to Talk to Your Dog, by Jean Craighead George

⸫ When to Use

After reading

⸫ Description of Strategy

A teacher selects key words from books that the students are reading and that exemplify particular phonic concepts or spelling patterns. Each student is given a set of individual alphabet letters. These may be written on cards or may be plastic letters. A sheet is provided to each student and has boxes on it representing the number of phonemes contained in each word. If a word has three phonemes, such as /dog/, three boxes are on the page, and the students are given no more than six letters to choose from. The teacher leads the students to "build" or spell a variety of words by "pushing" the letters or letter combinations into the appropriate sound box.

§ Procedures for Use

1. The teacher orally reads *How to Talk to Your Dog*.

2. After reading, the teacher explains that the students are going to use letters to build some words that are in the book. The teacher identifies words for study.

3. Each student has a sheet with three boxes drawn on it. Each student also has three alphabet letters that are the same size or smaller than the boxes. In this example, the word "dog" is selected. (See Figure 7–1.)

4. On an overhead projector, chart paper, or board, the teacher models how to listen to the sounds in the word "dog" by dragging out the voice as "dog" is pronounced. The teacher explains that three sounds are heard. The teacher might say, "I am looking for three letters that represent those sounds so that I can build or spell this word."

5. Slowly, the teacher slides a **d** into the first box. The students follow the lead. The same process occurs with the **o** and **g**. The teacher observes to be sure that each student has built the word correctly. The teacher and class then say the word slowly together as they track under the word with their fingers. Then the students say the word fast as they underline the word with their fingers.

6. The students remove the letters from the boxes, mix them up, and see whether they can "build" the word independently.

7. The teacher instructs the class to add a letter to the ones on the desk, so that each learner now has four letters—a **d**, **o**, **g**, and any other letter. In Figure 7–2 the letter **m** is added. It is best to select a letter that is configured differently from the ones in the word "dog." For example, **p**, **q**, or **b** would be poor choices because they look similar to **d** or **g**. After these letters are mixed up, the students see whether they can still spell "dog" with the extraneous letter **m** not being used.

8. Depending on the level of the class, the teacher may advance the activity to initial consonant substitutions, then to final consonant substitutions, then to vowel substitutions. (See the example that follows in Figure 7–3 where **t** replaces **g** at the end of the word to form "dot.")

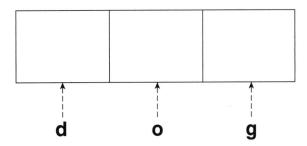

FIGURE 7–1   Example of Word Building Boxes with *How to Talk to Your Dog*

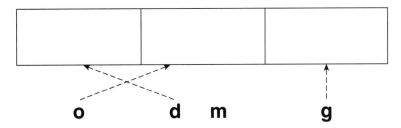

FIGURE 7–2   Example of Word Building Boxes with an Extraneous Letter from *How to Talk to Your Dog*

Initial Constant Substitutions	Final Consonant Substitutions	Vowel Substitutions
dog log hog	dot	
fun sun bun pun ————————————→	pup ————————————→	pan pin pen
mad sad bad had ————————————→	hat ————————————→ ham ————————————→ had ————————————→ has ————————————→	hit him hid his

FIGURE 7–3 Examples of Word Building with Initial Consonants, Final Consonants, and Vowel Substitutions
Note: If the word being built requires a combination of letters to represent a phoneme, one of the boxes will need a dotted line. In the following example with "tell," the two "l's" are one grapheme representing one phoneme.

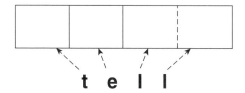

FURTHER READING

Frey, N., & Fisher, D. (2006). *Language arts workshop: Purposeful reading and writing instruction.* Columbus, OH: Pearson Prentice Hall.

Gipe, J. P. (2006). *Multiple paths to literacy: Assessment and differentiated instruction for diverse learners, K–12* (6th ed.). Upper Saddle River, NJ: Merrill/Prentice Hall.

Johns, J., & Lenski, S. D. (2001). *Improving reading: Strategies and resources* (3rd ed.). Dubuque, IA: Kendall/Hunt.

Multiple Word Meaning Matching Game

EL *Also beneficial when working with English learners*

Strategy at a Glance: *Grade Levels 1–8*

When to Use	Grouping	Literature Type	Skill Areas
○ before reading	● individual	● narrative	● word recognition
○ during reading	○ small group	○ expository	○ vocabulary
● after reading	○ whole class		● comprehension
	● center		○ writing

Purpose

To teach the literal and inferred meanings of multiple word meaning phrases

Literature Used

Play Ball, Amelia Bedelia, by Peggy Parish

When to Use

After reading

Description of Strategy

This strategy will help students seek literal and inferred meanings of phrases that have more than one meaning. The teacher writes these phrases from the story with multiple meanings on cards that are cut to be the same size. During the activity, the student will match the phrase on one card with the match of its meaning from the story on another card.

Procedures for Use

1. *After* reading the story *Play Ball, Amelia Bedelia,* the teacher discusses the multiple word meaning phrases presented in the story. The teacher reviews the literal and inferred meanings of each phrase with students. For example, "Run home, Amelia Bedelia" in this story context means that Amelia should run to home base, not run to her house. By understanding the different meanings of the words, the reader can catch the humor of Amelia Bedelia stories, since Amelia always chooses the wrong or unintended definition of words or phrases.

2. Once readers seem to understand the phrases, the teacher sets up cards face down on the table. The teacher then explains that the activity is similar to the game of matching.

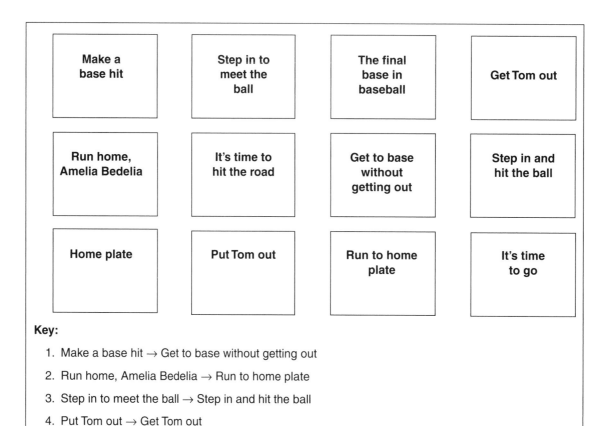

Make a base hit	Step in to meet the ball	The final base in baseball	Get Tom out
Run home, Amelia Bedelia	It's time to hit the road	Get to base without getting out	Step in and hit the ball
Home plate	Put Tom out	Run to home plate	It's time to go

Key:

1. Make a base hit → Get to base without getting out

2. Run home, Amelia Bedelia → Run to home plate

3. Step in to meet the ball → Step in and hit the ball

4. Put Tom out → Get Tom out

5. Home plate → The final base in baseball

6. It's time to hit the road → It's time to go

FIGURE 8–1 Example from *Play Ball, Amelia Bedelia*

3. The student picks up one card and reads what it says. The student flips over another card and reads what it says. Figure 8–1 illustrates possible phrases from *Play Ball, Amelia Bedelia* and their matching definitions.

4. If the two cards flipped are the phrase and the meaning of that phrase, as used in this story, the student keeps the two cards and continues to match.

    Example of two cards that match:
        Card 1: "Run home, Amelia Bedelia"
        Card 2: "Run to home plate"

If these two cards do not match, the student turns both cards over and repeats the process until two cards do match.

5. If students understand the concept of multiple word meanings, the teacher could apply it to a similar activity in a literacy center. The students might work in pairs and take turns matching the phrases.

FURTHER READING

Gipe, J. P. (2006). *Multiple paths to literacy: Assessment and differentiated instruction for diverse learners, K–12* (6th ed.). Upper Saddle River, NJ: Merrill/Prentice Hall.

Gunning, T. (2005). *Creating literacy instruction for all students* (5th ed.). Boston: Allyn & Bacon.

9

Word Detective Cards

 Also beneficial when working with English learners

Strategy at a Glance: *Grade Levels 1–3*			
When to Use	**Grouping**	**Literature Type**	**Skill Areas**
● before reading	● individual	● narrative	● word recognition
● during reading	● small group	● expository	○ vocabulary
● after reading	● whole class		○ comprehension
	○ center		○ writing

Purpose

To help students become independent readers by learning strategies effective readers use to decode unknown words

Literature Used

The Puppy Who Wanted a Boy, by Jane Thayer

When to Use

Before, during, and after reading

Description of Strategy

Word detective cards present four word recognition strategies, one on each card, that efficient readers use when they come to an unknown word. Each of the four cards has directions for a reader to apply in decoding an unknown word by selecting from a variety of word attack competencies: context clues, structural analysis, phonics, and use of a dictionary.

Procedures for Use

1. The teacher selects a short passage with several words that the readers cannot automatically pronounce. In this example, the passage was from *The Puppy Who Wanted a Boy*. The words selected were "puppy," "dog," "I'd," and "Christmas." (See Figure 9–1.) The teacher writes individual sentences from the passage on sentence strips.

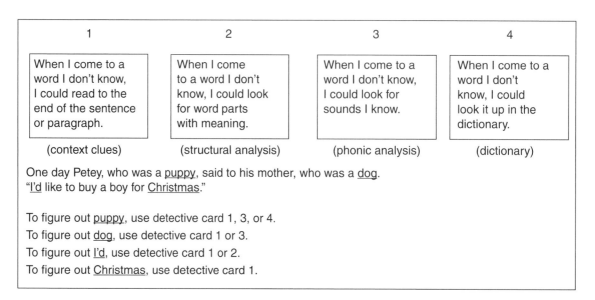

1	2	3	4
When I come to a word I don't know, I could read to the end of the sentence or paragraph.	When I come to a word I don't know, I could look for word parts with meaning.	When I come to a word I don't know, I could look for sounds I know.	When I come to a word I don't know, I could look it up in the dictionary.
(context clues)	(structural analysis)	(phonic analysis)	(dictionary)

One day Petey, who was a <u>puppy</u>, said to his mother, who was a <u>dog</u>. "<u>I'd</u> like to buy a boy for <u>Christmas</u>."

To figure out <u>puppy</u>, use detective card 1, 3, or 4.
To figure out <u>dog</u>, use detective card 1 or 3.
To figure out <u>I'd</u>, use detective card 1 or 2.
To figure out <u>Christmas</u>, use detective card 1.

FIGURE 9–1   Example of Word Detective Cards with *The Puppy Who Wanted a Boy*

2. The teacher asks the students whether they know what a detective is. If not, the teacher explains that a detective is someone who uses clues to figure out mysteries. The teacher tells the students that they will serve as word detectives and use clues to figure out the mystery of unknown words.

3. The teacher has the students to read the individual sentences silently and underline any unknown words.

4. The teacher asks the students to reread the sentence out loud, saying "blank" when an unknown word appears.

5. The teacher shows the readers the first word detective card. The teacher reads the first word detective card to the students and asks whether the suggestion on that card will help to figure out the mystery of the word. (See Figure 9–1.)

6. If the first card does not help the student, the teacher will flip to the second card, then the third, then the fourth if necessary. **The order of the cards is very important!** The cards should be presented in the order in which efficient readers attempt to pronounce unknown words, starting with context clues, until the reader successfully reads the word. For example, if the unknown word is "puppy," the first detective card might be used. If the reader knows the word "dog" later in the sentence, the reader applies context clues to pronounce "puppy." The third detective card might be used next if the first clue didn't help, to break "puppy" into sound units, /pup/ /py/. Or the student might look the word "puppy" up in the dictionary, as the fourth card suggests.

7. The teacher may manipulate the cards to cover and uncover word parts to assist the students if they are dividing the word by structural or meaning units (the second card) or phonic or sound units (the third card).

8. The teacher will provide scaffolding as readers try to engage in the various word attack skills. If the student is trying to sound out the word "puppy," the teacher might help by showing the student how the word is divided into syllables and more easily pronounced as opposed to trying to blend isolated sounds.

9. Once the word has been identified, the teacher should ask the students whether the "guess" makes sense in the sentence.

FURTHER READING

Cooper, J. D. (2000). *Literacy: Helping children construct meaning* (4th ed.). Boston: Houghton Mifflin.

Tompkins, G. E. (2006). *Literacy for the 21st century: A balanced approach* (4th ed.). Upper Saddle River, NJ: Merrill/Prentice Hall.

10 VAKT for Sight Word Recognition and Spelling

(EL) *Also beneficial when working with English learners*

Strategy at a Glance: *Grade Levels All*

When to Use	Grouping	Literature Type	Skill Areas
● before reading	● individual	● narrative	● word recognition
● during reading	○ small group	● expository	○ vocabulary
● after reading	○ whole class		○ comprehension
	● center		○ writing

Purpose

To enhance sight word recognition, fluency, and correct spelling of words that are difficult to learn

---

Literature Used

Sector 7, by David Wiesner

When to Use

Before, during, and after reading

Description of Strategy

Developed by Grace Fernald and Helen Keller, VAKT (visual, auditory, kinesthetic, tactile) is an approach that improves recognition of sight words and increases spelling ability. The technique derives its power from the use of multiple modalities of learning. For a word that is difficult to establish as a sight word, the teacher shows the reader the word printed in letters large enough to be traced. The target word should have a raised or rough surface so that the reader can feel it as it is traced. A crayon works well for a raised, textured surface, or the word card may be inserted into a sleeve made by folding a mesh screen so that a rough surface is available for the reader to trace over. (See Figure 10–1.)

FIGURE 10–1   Example of Mesh Screen
Sleeve and Word Card

An important consideration with this strategy is that the target word **not** be taught in isolation from a meaningful context. The word should derive from a narrative or expository passage students are reading. A further way to make the word meaningful is for the teacher or student to use it in a sentence during the following procedures.

⑧ Procedures for Use

1. To develop sight word fluency with a student, the teacher may select a book like *Sector 7,* a wordless picture storybook by David Wiesner. The book is shared with the student for a follow-up language experience story. (Refer to Strategy 5, Language Experience Approach for Sight Word Development.)

2. Once *Sector 7* has been shared and discussed, the student dictates to the teacher a short language experience story for a part of the book. The teacher and student then read the story in the shared reading mode of read *aloud, along, alone*. When the student independently reads the story *alone,* the teacher will note words that prove to be difficult for the student to pronounce automatically such as the word "where." The teacher could then employ VAKT as an *after* reading intervention to establish "where" as a sight word.

3. Using an index card, the teacher prints "where" in large letters for the student to trace:

where

   The teacher pronounces the word and says it slowly as the student watches it being printed. Upon completing the printing, the teacher repeats the word in a normal voice and underlines it with a finger as the student looks at the word. The teacher next asks the student to look at the word and say it.

4. The teacher places the word card in a mesh screen to give it a textured surface over which to trace. (See Figure 10–1.) While looking at the word again, the student slowly pronounces "where" by stretching it out with the voice and at the same time tracing over the letters. Thus, the student sees the word, hears the word, and feels the word as part of the auditory, visual, and tactile components of VAKT.

5. The process continues until the student is able to write the word successfully from memory several times. The word card is then placed alphabetically in the reader's

FIGURE 10–2   Example of a Water Pen with Sponge Tip

individual file box or "word bank" for later retrieval if it continues to prove troublesome when encountered in print.

6. Had the reader needed additional practice with "where" or a more intense intervention to establish it as a sight word, the teacher could have tried a water pen. This is a hollow plastic tube with a small sponge on the end used for dampening seals on envelopes. (See Figure 10–2.)

This instrument aids the reader in remembering sight words by adding the kinesthetic component of VAKT. The student can trace the word on a chalkboard with the damp sponge tip of the water pen and thereby use large muscle movement as an additional learning modality. Again, the reader should slowly pronounce the word as each letter is traced. An alternative to a water pen for kinesthetic and tracing methods is any damp sponge.

FURTHER READING

Fernald, G. (1943). *Remedial techniques in basic school subjects.* New York: McGraw-Hill.

Gipe, J. P. (2006). *Multiple paths to literacy: Assessment and differentiated instruction for diverse learners, K–12* (6th ed.). Upper Saddle River, NJ: Merrill/Prentice Hall.

Harris, A. J., & Sipay, E. R. (1990). *How to increase reading ability: A guide to developmental and remedial methods* (9th ed.). New York: Longman.

Norton, T., & Land, B. L. (1992). A multisensory approach to teaching spelling in remedial English. *Teaching English in the Two-Year College, 19,* 192–195.

PART III

Vocabulary Strategies

11 Semantic Feature Analysis for Narrative and Informational Text

 Also beneficial when working with English learners

Strategy at a Glance: *Grade Levels 1–2*			
When to Use	**Grouping**	**Literature Type**	**Skill Areas**
● before reading	● individual	● narrative	○ word recognition
● during reading	● small group	● expository	● vocabulary
● after reading	● whole class		● comprehension
	○ center		● writing

Purpose

To develop vocabulary proficiency by identifying word properties that may be similar or different from other words in a category and comparing and contrasting these concepts.

Literature Used

Pass the Fritters, Critters, by Cheryl Chapman (narrative)

Dinosaur Time, by Peggy Parish (expository)

When to Use

Before, during, and/or after reading

Description of Strategy

Semantic feature analysis uses a chart format to compare and contrast different characters, terms, or concepts from a book to help students with vocabulary development and a deeper understanding of concepts. A few words may be introduced *before* a selection is read, while others are added *during* reading, and still others *after* the passage or book is completed. The chart provides a helpful review of important concepts that the teacher wishes to emphasize to students. This process helps learners understand the deeper dimensions of the meanings of words.

⊗ Procedures for Use

1. A book or selection that is rich in terms related to one another works best. *Pass the Fritters, Critters,* by Cheryl Chapman, is a good example. *Dinosaur Time,* by Peggy Parish, has many vocabulary words that students can compare and contrast.

2. The teacher and students select key vocabulary from a book.

3. These items are then listed on the left-hand side of a grid or chart. In *Pass the Fritters, Critters,* students may select "muffin" and "cobbler." (See Figure 11–1.) In *Dinosaur Time,* the names of different dinosaurs may be listed on the left side of the grid (e.g., stegosaurus, diplodocus, ankylosaurus, etc.). (See Figure 11–2.)

4. With the teacher's assistance, students list the characteristics of selected terms and put these across the top of the grid.

5. Through student-teacher interactions, the items (foods or dinosaurs) from the book are then labeled as to which features they possess. A "+" indicates "yes" for a particular feature, while a "–" means "no" and a "?" means further investigation of other sources such as a dictionary or encyclopedia is necessary. A "+/–" means "yes" and "no," or that the food/dinosaur may or may not possess a given feature. Discussion among students or between the teacher and students is important to make sure that the learners understand that some terms are characterized by a feature and others are not.

6. Additional names and features may be placed on the grid as further reading and enrichment occurs.

7. Once the grid is completed, it serves as a review of the topic or unit of study, as can be seen from the samples of semantic feature analysis provided in Figures 11–1 and 11–2.

Alternate Idea

The basic chart may be created, and the concepts, attributes, and symbols (+, −, ?, +/−) may be added to the chart using self-stick notes. This idea is especially effective for

Food	Attributes				
	Sweet	Made with Fruit	Vegetable	Eaten Raw	Requires Utensil
fritters	+	+	−	−	−
cantalope	+	+	−	+	+/−
muffin	+	+	−	−	−
eclair	+	−	−	−	−
cobbler	+	+	−	−	+
honey	+	−	−	+	+/−
carrot	−	−	+	+/−	+/−
salami	−	−	−	+?	+/−
cider	+	+	−	+	+(glass)

+ = yes
− = no
? = need for further study
+/− = yes and no

FIGURE 11–1 Example for *Pass the Fritters, Critters*

Dinosaurs	Attributes			
	Meat-eater	Plant-eater	Smooth Body	Rough Body
stegosaurus	−	+	−	+
diplodocus	−	+	+	−
ankylosaurus	?	?	−	+
brontosaurus	−	+	−	+
compsognathus	+	−	+	−
teratosaurus	+	−	+	−
anatosaurus	?	?	−	+
ornithominus	+	+	+	−

+ = yes
− = no
? = need for further study
+/− = yes and no

FIGURE 11–2   Example for *Dinosaur Time*

tactile/kinesthetic learners. The chart may eventually be placed in a center, and the self-stick notes removed for the students to replace. Learners needing more practice or reinforcement will benefit from this idea.

FURTHER READING

Cooper, J. D. (2000). *Literacy: Helping children construct meaning* (4th ed.). Boston: Houghton Mifflin.

Cooter, R. B., Jr., & Flynt, E. S. (1996). *Teaching reading in the content areas: Developing content literacy for all students.* Englewood Cliffs, NJ: Prentice Hall.

Cunningham, P., & Allington, R. (1994). *Classrooms that work.* New York: HarperCollins.

Cunningham, P. M., Moore, S. A., Cunningham, J. W., & Moore, D. W. (1995). *Reading and writing in elementary classrooms: Strategies and observations* (3rd ed.). White Plains, NY: Longman.

Frey, N., & Fisher, D. (2006). *Language arts workshop: Purposeful reading and writing instruction.* Columbus, OH: Pearson Prentice Hall.

Gipe, J. P. (2006). *Multiple paths to literacy: Assessment and differentiated instruction for diverse learners, K–12* (6th ed.). Upper Saddle River, NJ: Merrill/Prentice Hall.

Graves, M., Juel, C., & Graves, B. (1998). *Teaching reading in the 21st century.* Needham Heights, MA: Allyn & Bacon.

Gunning, T. (2005). *Creating literacy instruction for all students* (5th ed.). Boston: Allyn & Bacon.

Harris, A. J., & Sipay, E. R. (1990). *How to increase reading ability: A guide to developmental and remedial methods* (9th ed.). New York: Longman.

Johns, J., & Lenski, S. D. (2001). *Improving reading: Strategies and resources* (3rd ed.). Dubuque, IA: Kendall/Hunt.

Reutzel, D. R., & Cooter, R. (2000). *Teaching children to read: Putting the pieces together* (3rd ed.). Columbus, OH: Merrill.

Vacca, R. T., & Vacca, J. A. L. (2005). *Content area reading: Literacy and learning across the curriculum* (8th ed.). Boston: Allyn & Bacon.

12 Concept of Definition or Word Map

(EL) *Also beneficial when working with English learners*

Strategy at a Glance: *Grade Levels 4–8*

When to Use	Grouping	Literature Type	Skill Areas
● before reading	○ individual	● narrative	○ word recognition
● during reading	● small group	● expository	● vocabulary
● after reading	● whole class		● comprehension
	○ center		● writing

Purpose

To activate background and expand vocabulary through an examination of the components of an analytical definition

Literature Used

Follow the Drinking Gourd, by Jeanette Winter

When to Use

Before, during, and/or after reading

Description of Strategy

Concept of definition, or word mapping, is a vocabulary development strategy that activates prior knowledge *before* reading or expands knowledge *during* and *after* reading. The technique uses a visual representation to show specific parts of a vocabulary concept. When the strategy is used *before* reading, key concept words must be selected prior to reading the literature selection. An example of the components associated with a word map is shown in Figure 12–1. *Before* reading, the teacher and students should discuss the vocabulary word, or key concept, and what the students know about it, such as some of its characteristics or some examples. This discussion activates background knowledge. Together, the teacher and students make a list of properties or examples related to the key concept. Some of the

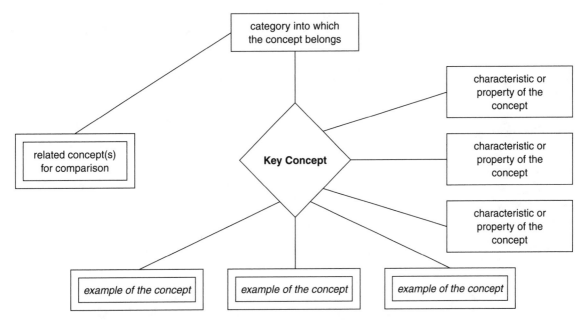

FIGURE 12–1   Example of Components Associated with a Word Map

characteristics or examples can be recorded on the map. *During* reading, these may be added to or changed. *After* reading, the teacher and students decide whether the definition is still incomplete and may search other sources for further information to complete the components of the definition. The following procedures illustrate the strategy for a children's book that could be used with intermediate- and middle-grade social studies.

Procedures for Use

1. The teacher introduces a key concept used in the book, *Follow the Drinking Gourd.* In this example, the concept is "slaves." This word is recorded in the center of the map. (Refer to the completed word map in Figure 12–2.)

2. The teacher and students next identify the category in which the concept "slaves" belongs. For instance, slaves may be classified as workers. "Workers" then goes at the top of the map.

3. Comparisons can now be made between "slaves" and similar concepts by listing other examples of "workers," such as "carpenters" and "farmers." These examples go to the left of the map as "Related Concept(s) for Comparison."

4. The teacher and students brainstorm and list characteristics or properties of "slaves." Examples may include "lived and worked on plantations," "abused and beaten," and "did not have freedom." Reader responses go to the right of the map in boxes labeled "Characteristics or Properties of the Concept."

5. Students next try to think of illustrations of "slaves." These may include such examples as "cotton pickers," "domestic (or house) workers," "field hands," and "skilled laborers." These terms go at the bottom of the map in the boxes labeled "Example of the Concept" and could be subdivided further. "House workers" could be divided, for instance, into "butlers," "maids," "cooks," and so forth.

6. As a follow-up, the concept may be formally written by having students arrange the map into a definition sentence or paragraph (in this instance, "slaves") based on the information given in the map. Responses and final definitions will vary based on background and further reading.

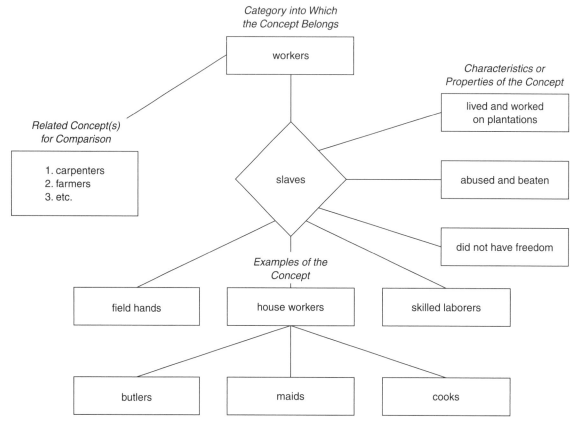

FIGURE 12–2 Example for *Follow the Drinking Gourd*

7. In summary, the basic process for concept of definition is to *list* ideas about a concept, *group* the ideas, and *label* the ideas as "Characteristics or Properties of the Concept," "Examples of the Concept," or "Related Concept(s) for Comparison."

FURTHER READING

Cooper, J. D. (2000). *Literacy: Helping children construct meaning* (4th ed.). Boston: Houghton Mifflin.

Frey, N., & Fisher, D. (2006). *Language arts workshop: Purposeful reading and writing instruction.* Columbus, OH: Pearson Prentice Hall.

Gipe, J. P. (2006). *Multiple paths to literacy: Assessment and differentiated instruction for diverse learners, K–12* (6th ed.). Upper Saddle River, NJ: Merrill/Prentice Hall.

Harris, A. J., & Sipay, E. R. (1990). *How to increase reading ability: A guide to developmental and remedial methods* (9th ed.). New York: Longman.

Johns, J., & Lenski, S. D. (2001). *Improving reading: Strategies and resources* (3rd ed.). Dubuque, IA: Kendall/Hunt.

Reutzel, D. R., & Cooter, R. (2000). *Teaching children to read: Putting the pieces together* (3rd ed.). Columbus, OH: Merrill.

Ruddell, R. B., & Ruddell, M. R. (1995). *Teaching children to read and write: Becoming an influential teacher.* Boston: Allyn & Bacon.

Tierney, R. J., & Readence, J. E. (2000). *Reading strategies and practices: A compendium* (5th ed.). Boston: Allyn & Bacon.

Vacca, J. A. L., Vacca, R. T., & Gove, M. K. (2000). *Reading and learning to read* (4th ed.). New York: Addison Wesley Longman.

Vacca, R. T., & Vacca, J. A. L. (2005). *Content area reading: Literacy and learning across the curriculum* (8th ed.). Boston: Allyn & Bacon.

13 Venn Diagram for Comparison-Contrast

(EL) *Also beneficial when working with English learners*

Strategy at a Glance: *Grade Levels All*

When to Use	Grouping	Skill Areas	Literature Type
○ before reading	○ individual	● narrative	● word recognition
● during reading	● small group	● expository	● vocabulary
● after reading	● whole class		● comprehension
	○ center		● writing

Purpose

To compare and contrast two things (e.g., two books, two settings, two characters within a book, and so on)

Literature Used

Next Year I'll Be Special, by Patricia Reilly Giff

When to Use

During or after reading

Description of Strategy

A Venn diagram compares and contrasts two different items and is illustrated by overlapping circles. (Some Venn diagrams may be used for three items but are often too complicated. For three or more items, a version of a semantic feature analysis might work better. (See pages 37–39.) Each circle represents one of the two items. The common characteristics are written in the space where the two circles overlap. The different characteristics of the items are written on the inside of the separate parts of each circle that represents the item. The example for *Next Year I'll Be Special* in Figure 13–1 provides an illustration.

Procedures for Use

1. The basic process of this strategy is to *list* ideas, *group* them, and categorize them under the *labels* given (e.g., reality and imagination) as the subsequent procedures illustrate.

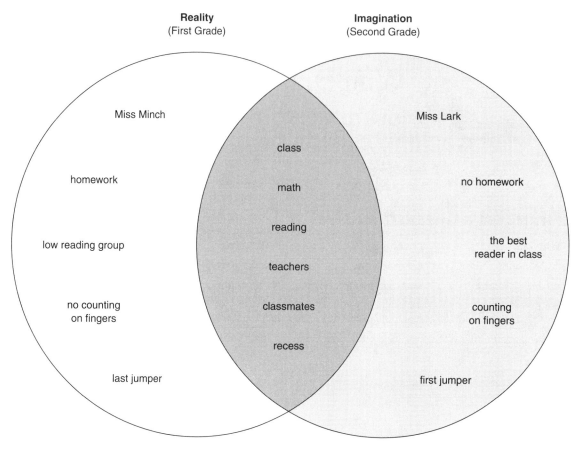

FIGURE 13–1   Example for *Next Year I'll Be Special*

2. *After* one or several readings of *Next Year I'll Be Special,* students compile or brainstorm a list of Marilyn's (the main character's) first-grade realities and her imagined second-grade experiences.

3. Two overlapping medium-sized circles are drawn in which to write the items from the compiled *list.* Before writing in the circles, the students and teacher should compare and contrast the list of characteristics for the first and second grades to verify the sections of the circles in which they should be written.

4. Students next should *group* the common characteristics by writing them in the overlapping part of the two circles.

5. Students should now write the differences between first and second grades in the separate parts of the two circles, so that individual characteristics are now *labeled* as "reality," "imagination," or both. (Thus, first-grade characteristics are grouped on the side of the first-grade circle, and second-grade characteristics are grouped on the side of the second-grade circle in Figure 13–1.)

6. The teacher should follow up by discussing each part of the circle with the students. If a characteristic is not in the correct part of the diagram, they should decide where to place the characteristic.

7. The Venn diagram also may be used as a prewriting activity to help students organize their ideas for comparing and contrasting the reality of first grade with Marilyn's imagined second grade. In this case, the Venn diagram serves as an outline in which students have organized their thoughts before they begin writing a draft.

8. The Venn diagram is an excellent strategy for reading comprehension competencies like comparison-contrast or categorization as well as for vocabulary development and prewriting.

FURTHER READING

Cooper, J. D. (2000). *Literacy: Helping children construct meaning* (4th ed.). Boston: Houghton Mifflin.

Cunningham, P., & Allington, R. (1994). *Classrooms that work.* New York: HarperCollins.

Graves, M., Juel, C., & Graves, B. (1998). *Teaching reading in the 21st century.* Needham Heights, MA: Allyn & Bacon.

Gunning, T. (2005). *Creating literacy instruction for all students* (5th ed.). Boston: Allyn & Bacon.

Harris, A. J., & Sipay, E. R. (1990). *How to increase reading ability: A guide to developmental and remedial methods* (9th ed.). New York: Longman.

Johns, J., & Lenski, S. D. (2001). *Improving reading: Strategies and resources* (3rd ed.). Dubuque, IA: Kendall/Hunt.

Tierney, R. J., & Readence, J. E. (2000). *Reading strategies and practices: A compendium* (5th ed.). Boston: Allyn & Bacon.

Tompkins, G. E. (2005). *Language arts: Patterns of practice* (6th ed.). Upper Saddle River, NJ: Merrill/Prentice Hall.

Vacca, R. T., & Vacca, J. A. L. (2005). *Content area reading: Literacy and learning across the curriculum* (8th ed.). Boston: Allyn & Bacon.

14 Thinking Tree

Strategy at a Glance: *Grade Levels All*			
When to Use	**Grouping**	**Literature Type**	**Skill Areas**
⬭ before reading	⬭ individual	⬤ narrative	⬭ word recognition
⬭ during reading	⬤ small group	⬤ expository	⬤ vocabulary
⬤ after reading	⬤ whole class		⬤ comprehension
	⬭ center		⬤ writing

Purpose

To show the hierarchical relationships among vocabulary terms or among main ideas and details through the use of a graphic organizer

Literature Used

The News about Dinosaurs, by Patricia Lauber

When to Use

After reading

Description of Strategy

A thinking tree is an instructional tool to help students organize information into categories that are hierarchically arranged. Depending on learner needs and abilities, thinking trees can be modified. A thinking tree starts with a broad category at the top of the tree chart. Students can select this category, be supplied with the category, or choose the category from a given concept bank. As the tree chart moves down, the categories get more specific. Each category describes in greater detail the category above it. The tree chart also expands horizontally each time it moves down. Thus, a thinking tree contains superordinate, subordinate, and coordinate items. The chart may initially provide some of the superordinate, subordinate, and coordinate concepts so that students fill in the remaining items themselves, or students may choose from a concept bank provided by the teacher. The teacher decides how the thinking trees will be filled in and how much scaffolding, or assistance, is needed.

Procedures for Use

1. The literature selected for this thinking tree is *The News about Dinosaurs.*

2. *After* the literature has been read either in an independent or a shared mode such as read *aloud, along,* or *alone,* the teacher provides a random list of topics that students later arrange hierarchically into a thinking tree. Alternatively, the teacher may guide the students in generating a list of concepts from the text.

3. The concepts, whether from the teacher, from students, or from both, are then arranged into a thinking tree that shows superordinate, subordinate, or coordinate relationships. For less able students, the tree chart may be provided. Others may create their own. The degree of scaffolding provided by the teacher is dependent upon the individual needs of learners.

4. For *The News about Dinosaurs,* the teacher has provided the thinking tree and a list of terms in a concept bank. (See Figure 14–1.) The superordinate concept is "dinosaurs." Subordinate to it and coordinate with each other are "plant-eaters" and "meat-eaters." Then subordinate to these and coordinate with one another are examples of different dinosaurs.

5. From the concept bank, students hierarchically order the terms from *The News about Dinosaurs.* This work may be done independently, cooperatively, or with teacher guidance. Moreover, the teacher may have some sections of the thinking tree already completed if this degree of scaffolding is necessary for particular students. (See Figure 14–1.)

6. Depending on the student, a thinking tree may continue to expand or stop after one or two subordinate levels are completed.

7. The teacher may give several examples of thinking trees to lead students eventually to create their own thinking trees. Figure 14–2 provides a variation of Figure 14–1.

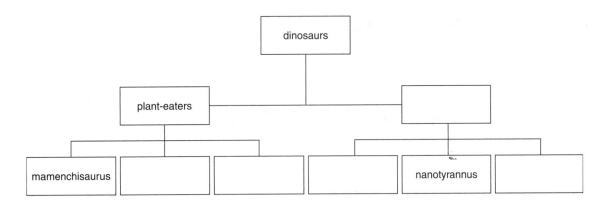

FIGURE 14–1   Example One for *The News about Dinosaurs*
Note: This thinking tree has some of the categories filled in to provide greater scaffolding to help the students decide what should go in the rest of the category boxes. This thinking tree also has a concept bank. Students will fill in the category boxes with words or names from this randomly ordered list.

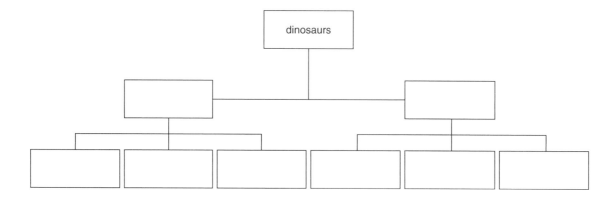

Concept Bank

plant-eaters
mamenchisaurus
deinonychus
meat-eaters
nanotyrannus
albertosaurus
camarasaurus
apatosaurus

FIGURE 14–2   Example Two for *The News about Dinosaurs*
Note: Some thinking trees may be like this one. The broad category is given, and the remaining thinking tree boxes have to be filled in by the student with words from the concept box. This type of thinking tree requires a higher level of application than does the first example. Thinking trees can expand.

FURTHER READING

Cooper, J. D. (2000). *Literacy: Helping children construct meaning* (4th ed.). Boston: Houghton Mifflin.

Cooter, R. B., Jr., & Flynt, E. S. (1996). *Teaching reading in the content areas: Developing content literacy for all students.* Englewood Cliffs, NJ: Prentice Hall.

Graves, M., Juel, C., & Graves, B. (1998). *Teaching reading in the 21st century.* Needham Heights, MA: Allyn & Bacon.

Gunning, T. (2005). *Creating literacy instruction for all students* (5th ed.). Boston: Allyn & Bacon.

Johns, J., & Lenski, S. D. (2001). *Improving reading: Strategies and resources* (3rd ed.). Dubuque, IA: Kendall/Hunt.

Reutzel, D. R., & Cooter, R. (2000). *Teaching children to read: Putting the pieces together* (3rd ed.). Columbus, OH: Merrill.

Vacca, R. T., & Vacca, J. A. L. (2005). *Content area reading: Literacy and learning across the curriculum* (8th ed.). Boston: Allyn & Bacon.

15

Semantic Mapping or Webbing

(EL) *Also beneficial when working with English learners*

Strategy at a Glance: *Grade Levels All*			
When to Use	**Grouping**	**Literature Type**	**Skill Areas**
● before reading	○ individual	● narrative	○ word recognition
● during reading	● small group	● expository	● vocabulary
● after reading	● whole class		● comprehension
	○ center		● writing

Purpose

To organize information through a graphic depiction of words, concepts, or ideas and to demonstrate their relationship to one another

Literature Used

I Can Be a Zookeeper, by James P. Rowan

When to Use

Before, during, and/or after reading

Description of Strategy

Semantic mapping or webbing is a visual organizational technique that displays ideas according to the way they relate to one another categorically. It may be used *before* reading to preview key vocabulary and to focus student attention on important concepts that will appear in the text. It may also be used *during* and *after* reading to reinforce or to expand vocabulary and thereby increase comprehension. Usually, a key concept is selected by the teacher and discussed to build or activate the prior background of learners. They may add characteristics of the key concept to the map. *During* reading, these may be further added or taken from the map as necessary. *After* reading, the teacher and students complete the map by adding any relevant information obtained from the literature. The steps that follow suggest how semantic mapping improves comprehension of *I Can Be a Zookeeper.*

Procedures for Use

1. The teacher introduces a key term in *I Can Be a Zookeeper*, in this instance "zookeeper," which is written in the center of the map.

2. *Before* reading, the teacher may read the title of the book and have students hypothesize what information it will contain. *I Can Be a Zookeeper* contains information about the job of a zookeeper. Students will learn some things that a zookeeper does. They can come up with a title for the semantic map. A good title for this map might be "Jobs of a Zookeeper." If students already know some of the jobs of a zookeeper, they may fill in some of the circles surrounding the term.

3. The teacher will read the book and direct students to pay close attention to the descriptions given. They clearly outline several jobs of a zookeeper.

4. Once the book is read, students will look at the information already placed in the map and will decide whether it is correct and should stay or whether it is incorrect and needs to be omitted or modified. Students will then recall as much information as possible from the book and fill in the remainder of the concept map.

5. After the information has been listed, the teacher should encourage learners to revise the map by grouping information into labeled subcategories with appropriate supporting details. Thus, semantic mapping will help students recall and organize information from the text as they develop vocabulary and classifying abilities. In Figure 15–1, the ideas

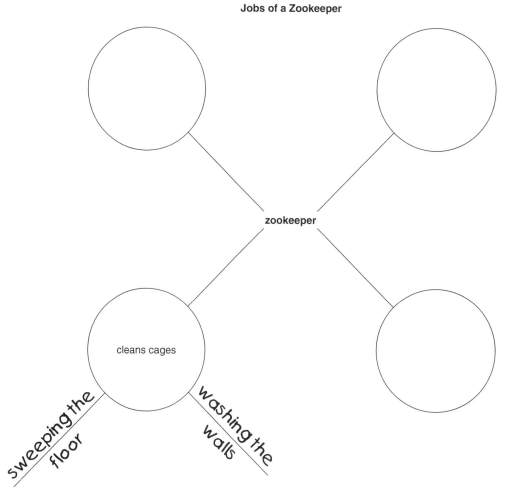

FIGURE 15–1   Example of a Semantic Web for *I Can Be a Zookeeper*

of "washing the walls" and "sweeping the floor" are attached to a larger category, "cleans cages."

6. The semantic web for *I Can Be a Zookeeper* can also be created as a fishbone to show students another way to organize the same ideas.

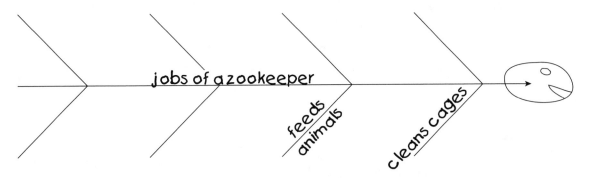

7. Using these kinds of graphic organizers, whether semantic mapping or a fishbone, gives learners a way to outline information as a prewriting activity for a written summary.

FURTHER READING

Cooper, J. D. (2000). *Literacy: Helping children construct meaning* (4th ed.). Boston: Houghton Mifflin.

Cunningham, P., & Allington, R. (1994). *Classrooms that work.* New York: HarperCollins.

Graves, M., Juel, C., & Graves, B. (1998). *Teaching reading in the 21st century.* Needham Heights, MA: Allyn & Bacon.

Gunning, T. (2005). *Creating literacy instruction for all students* (5th ed.). Boston: Allyn & Bacon.

Harris, A. J., & Sipay, E. R. (1990). *How to increase reading ability: A guide to developmental and remedial methods* (9th ed.). New York: Longman.

Johns, J., & Lenski, S. D. (2001). *Improving reading: Strategies and resources* (3rd ed.). Dubuque, IA: Kendall/Hunt.

Reutzel, D. R., & Cooter, R. (2000). *Teaching children to read: Putting the pieces together* (3rd ed.). Columbus, OH: Merrill.

Ruddell, R. B., & Ruddell, M. R. (1995). *Teaching children to read and write: Becoming an influential teacher.* Boston: Allyn & Bacon.

Vacca, J. A. L., Vacca, R. T., & Gove, M. K. (2000). *Reading and learning to read* (4th ed.). New York: Addison Wesley Longman.

Vacca, R. T., & Vacca, J. A. L. (2005). *Content area reading: Literacy and learning across the curriculum* (8th ed.). Boston: Allyn & Bacon.

16 Magic Squares

Strategy at a Glance: *Grade Levels All*

When to Use	Grouping	Literature Type	Skill Areas
○ before reading	● individual	● narrative	● word recognition
○ during reading	● small group	● expository	● vocabulary
● after reading	○ whole class		● comprehension
	○ center		○ writing

Purpose

To review key vocabulary terms for a lesson or unit of study whether based on narrative or expository text

Literature Used

South Carolina: Its History and Geography, by Paul Horne, Jr.

When to Use

After reading

Description of Strategy

Magic squares is a vocabulary reinforcement activity that gives additional exposure to terms *after* reading is completed. Students match key vocabulary words to their correct definitions. The activity, however, goes beyond a humdrum matching exercise in that it is like a game in which students record answers in a magic square grid made up of boxes like the one in Figure 16–1.

Each letter in the grid represents a term where learners write the number of the definition that matches. If they have correctly completed the activity, the numbers of the definitions, when added across each row and down each column, will equal the same "magic" number. Thus, the activity allows students to check their work for the accuracy of the matches.

A	B	C
D	E	F
G	H	I

Magic
Number = _____

FIGURE 16–1   Answer Grid

Magic squares work well with individual students or in small collaborative learning groups. The latter is particularly effective in reinforcing vocabulary words as students read the terms and definitions and engage in talking about them and hearing them through cooperative discussion.

Procedures for Use

1. The teacher should decide, *before* a lesson or unit is taught, the key terms that students should know and that support important learning outcomes.

2. The teacher should preview some of the terms *before,* and call attention to them *during,* the lesson to provide multiple exposures. This process is necessary for especially difficult concepts like the state motto of South Carolina, "Dum Spiro Spero."

3. *After* reading, reinforcement of terms and definitions for further exposure can occur with the magic squares activity. The example for *South Carolina: Its History and Geography,* an elementary social studies text, provides a review for nine key terms related to facts and symbols associated with South Carolina. (See Figure 16–4.)

4. To prevent the teacher from having to invent various magic square combinations, a time-consuming endeavor, additional ones are provided in Figure 16–2. The number with the single asterisk under each grid represents how many definitions must be foils, while the number with the double asterisk is the magic number that each row and column should sum up to if the exercise has been completed correctly.

5. Further magic square grids can be easily made by taking any one of the previous patterns and reconfiguring rows or columns. (See Figures 16–3 through 16–5.)

7	3	5
2	4	9
6	8	1

0*   15**

10	8	6
2	9	13
12	7	5

4*   24**

7	11	8
10	12	4
9	3	14

5*   26**

9	2	7
4	6	8
5	10	3

1*   18**

9	7	5
1	8	12
11	6	4

3*   21**

16	2	3	13
5	11	10	8
9	7	6	12
4	14	15	1

0*   34**

2	7	18	12
8	5	11	15
13	17	6	3
16	10	4	9

2*   39**

19	2	15	23	6
25	8	16	4	12
1	14	22	10	18
7	20	3	11	24
13	21	9	17	5

0*   65**

*foils for answer column with definitions
**magic number

FIGURE 16–2 Magic Square Combinations

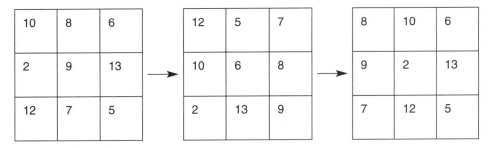

10	8	6
2	9	13
12	7	5

→

12	5	7
10	6	8
2	13	9

→

8	10	6
9	2	13
7	12	5

FIGURE 16–3   More Magic Square Combinations

Directions: We have just finished a unit about facts and symbols associated with South Carolina. We have covered a lot of information, and this activity can help you remember some of the vocabulary words from the unit.

Directions:

1. Look at the lists below. One list has vocabulary words from our unit. The other list has the definitions for the words.

2. Do you see the square at the bottom of the page? In the square, there are nine smaller squares with letters in them. The letters stand for the vocabulary words in our unit.

3. Write the number at the definition that matches in the proper square. Look at the example before you begin work.

4. The rows that go up and down and from side to side should all add up to be the same number. If this happens, you have probably gotten all of the definitions right.

5. Do your best!

Example:

Vocabulary List
A. Dog
B. Cat

Definition List
1. an animal that barks
2. an animal that meows

A	B
1	2

Exercise:

Vocabulary List

A. capital
B. Carolina jessamine
C. palmetto
D. "dum spiro spero"
E. milk
F. symbol
G. shag
H. Carolina wren
I. state flag

Definition List

1. Myrtle Beach
2. state motto
3. state song
4. state stone
5. designed by Colonel William Moultrie
6. state tree
7. state bird
8. state flower
9. state drink
10. where state government is located
11. is located on the coast
12. state dance
13. one thing that stands for another

A	B	C
D	E	F
G	H	I

Magic
Number = _____

FIGURE 16–4   Example for *South Carolina: Its History and Geography*

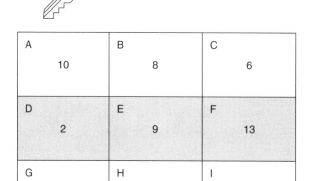

Magic Square
Answer Key

A 10	B 8	C 6
D 2	E 9	F 13
G 12	H 7	I 5

Magic Number = <u>24</u>

*Definition numbers 1, 3, 4, and 11 are foils
or incorrect answers.

FIGURE 16–5   Magic Square Answer Key

FURTHER READING

Vacca, R. T., & Vacca, J. A. L. (2005). *Content area reading: Literacy and learning across the curriculum* (8th ed.). Boston: Allyn & Bacon.

17 Context Puzzles

Strategy at a Glance: *Grade Levels All*			
When to Use	**Grouping**	**Literature Type**	**Skill Areas**
○ before reading	● individual	● narrative	● word recognition
○ during reading	● small group	● expository	● vocabulary
● after reading	○ whole class		● comprehension
	○ center		○ writing

Purpose

To reinforce knowledge of important vocabulary by having students use words in a meaningful context

Literature Used

Practical Record Keeping and Bookkeeping, by Harold Baron, Solomon C. Steinfeld, and Robert A. Schultheis

Art in Action, by Guy Hubbard

When to Use

After reading

Description of Strategy

Context puzzles are a variation of word puzzles. Unlike word puzzles, however, which give students definitions as clues, context puzzles require learners to apply vocabulary knowledge in a functional context. Students must use syntactic and semantic clues to determine the correct answer. Context puzzles are formatted as fill-in-the-blank activities and may consist of one sentence for each term or several connected sentences from a passage rich in vocabulary, particularly technical words found in content texts of an expository nature. The latter is a modified cloze puzzle having deletions of subject matter words as opposed to an *n*th (e.g., fifth) word deletion pattern. The teacher may scaffold these activities through letter clues; structural clues such as syllables, prefixes, and suffixes; or a blank space for each omitted letter of the term in question. Context puzzles may be completed in collaborative learning teams that require students to talk about terms, hear them, read them, and write them for additional reinforcement of learning.

Procedures for Use

1. A passage containing important vocabulary, often many technical terms, is ideal for a context puzzle to provide learners with review and practice using the words *after* reading. Examples from a unit on balancing a checkbook from *Practical Record Keeping and Bookkeeping* for a secondary business class and a unit on one-color collages from *Art in Action* for fifth-grade art are provided in Figures 17–1 and 17–2, respectively.

2. For the business puzzle, the teacher uses individual sentences that require learners to place each term in a meaningful context. The teacher must be sure that the sentences do indeed contain context clues. Otherwise, students will have too great a difficulty with the task because they cannot decipher the meanings of terms unless the context is adequate. The example for *Practical Record Keeping and Bookkeeping* shown in Figure 17–1 contains scaffolding with blanks for omitted letters and with some letters filled in. A word bank could also aid less able learners.

3. With the modified cloze puzzle for art, the teacher types a one-inch blank for each omitted word. This way, students must answer based on context, not on typographical clues. Unlike a cloze procedure used *before* reading assessment, a modified cloze puzzle does not employ a random deletion pattern for every *n*th word (usually every fifth word). Instead, this activity deletes only key vocabulary with which students need additional practice. The teacher could further scaffold this puzzle through letter, syllable, or affix clues in the blanks or through a concept bank from which students select answers. It all depends on the ability of the learners as to how much guidance the teacher gives them.

Directions: Use the sentences below, which contain clues for the meanings of words that we have from our unit on balancing a checkbook. Additional clues are provided with blanks for letters omitted from each term. In some cases, missing letters are given.

1. Banks can require customers to pay a s __ r __ __ __ e   c h __ __ __ __ for handling their deposits or for paying for their checks.

2. Sam went to his bank and made a __ __ t h __ __ __ __ __ l of $500 in cash to pay for a new paint job on his truck.

3. In order to __ __ __ __ __ __ __ i l e her checkbook with her bank statement, Susy had to determine that the balance in her checkbook matched her bank statement.

4. Susy used her __ __ __ __   __ __ c o n __ __ __ __ __ __ __ __   n s t __ __ __ __ __ __ t to see whether her check to the grocery store matched the amount recorded on her monthly statement from her bank.

5. When Jim received his paycheck in September, he recorded the amount in his checkbook. However, his bank statement for August did not show the amount of this __ __ __ s t __ __ i n g   d __ __ __ __ __ __ .

6. On June 1, Jim wrote a check for $30 to Home Depot for gardening tools he had purchased. His bank statement, dated May 28, will not show his __ __ __ __ __ __ e d   b __ __ __ __ __ __ for his June check.

Key:

1. service charge
2. withdrawal
3. reconcile

4. bank reconciliation statement
5. outstanding deposit
6. adjusted balance

FIGURE 17–1   Example for *Practical Record Keeping and Bookkeeping*

Directions: You have studied the section titled "One-Color Collage." From your text, you should have learned terms related to your reading as well as the artwork you created in class. You are required to fill in the missing words in this passage. Carefully read the content of the sentences because they contain clues to your answers.

Have you ever looked at the world through red-tinted glasses? Everything seems to show up as [1]____ of red. When something appears to be one color, we say that it is [2]____ . Colors, or [3]____ , can be changed in many ways. Adding black, white, or gray is a common way to change a color. You can add black to a color and make a [4]____ . You can add white and make a [5]____ . When you add gray to a color, you make a [6]____ . Pablo Picasso painted an all-blue painting called "The Blind Man's Meal." By repeating and varying the same color, you were asked to create a [8]____ . This is a [9]____ design made of materials such as paper and fabrics glued to a flat background. In creating your non-objective art, you were asked to use [10]____ shapes.

Key:

1. variations
2. monochrome or monochromatic
3. hues
4. shade
5. tint
6. tone
7. unity
8. collage
9. two-dimensional
10. geometric or free-form

FIGURE 17–2   Example for *Art in Action*

FURTHER READING

Cunningham, P. (2000). *Phonics they use* (3rd ed.). New York: Longman.

Gunning, T. (2005). *Creating literacy instruction for all students* (5th ed.). Boston: Allyn & Bacon.

Johns, J., & Lenski, S. D. (2001). *Improving reading: Strategies and resources* (3rd ed.). Dubuque, IA: Kendall/Hunt.

Reutzel, D. R., & Cooter, R. (2000). *Teaching children to read: Putting the pieces together* (3rd ed.). Columbus, OH: Merrill.

Ruddell, R. B., & Ruddell, M. R. (1995). *Teaching children to read and write: Becoming an influential teacher.* Boston: Allyn & Bacon.

Tierney, R. J., & Readence, J. E. (2000). *Reading strategies and practices: A compendium* (5th ed.). Boston: Allyn & Bacon.

Vacca, J. A. L., Vacca, R. T., & Gove, M. K. (2000). *Reading and learning to read* (4th ed.). New York: Addison Wesley Longman.

Vacca, R. T., & Vacca, J. A. L. (2005). *Content area reading: Literacy and learning across the curriculum* (8th ed.). Boston: Allyn & Bacon.

18 Closed and Open Word Sorts

(EL) *Also beneficial when working with English learners*

Strategy at a Glance: *Grade Levels All*

When to Use	Grouping	Literature Type	Skill Areas
○ before reading	● individual	● narrative	○ word recognition
○ during reading	● small group	● expository	● vocabulary
● after reading	● whole class		● comprehension
	○ center		○ writing

Purpose

To reinforce interrelationships among words and their meanings from an instructional unit so that students understand categories, properties, and examples of important terms

Literature Used

Holt Life Science, by Patricia A. Watkins and Glenn K. Leto

The Story of America, by John A. Garraty

When to Use

After reading

Description of Strategy

Students sort terms into different categorical groups through determining common features among their meanings. In closed sorts, the teacher provides the categories under which students are to group a given set of words. Here, the thinking is convergent and based on deduction. In open sorts, the students themselves group the given words into logical categories that they create based on previous reading and study. With open sorts, the thinking may be divergent since the word groupings are based on induction.

Procedures for Use

1. For a closed sort, the teacher searches the chapter, "Support and Movement," from *Holt Life Science* for middle-level learners and determines the key vocabulary on which to focus attention *before* and *during* reading. These words become the concept bank for students in the closed sort reinforcement of vocabulary *after* reading. (See Figure 18–1.) The same process applies to a senior high open sort activity for the chapter, "The Civil War," from *The Story of America.* (See Figure 18–2.) Both activities use a graphic organizer (i.e., a hierarchical array) to show connections among classes, properties, and examples.

2. In the closed sort, the teacher determines the major categories students will use to group the words and supplies these categories in the concept bank. In the one for *Holt Life Science,* the superordinate classes are "skeletal system" and "muscular system." Subordinate categories for "muscular system" have also been listed and are "skeletal muscles," "smooth muscles," and "cardiac muscles." For scaffolding, two of these are written on the graphic organizer. Thus, the teacher has completed

Directions: Choose the correct word or phrase from the concept bank below for each empty space on the graphic organizer. Only one word or phrase belongs in each space. Remember to write neatly.

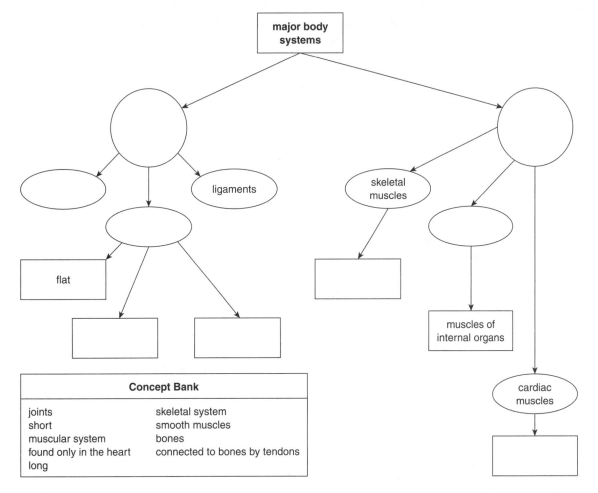

FIGURE 18–1 Example of Closed Sort for *Holt Life Science*
Note: This graphic organizer has some of the categories filled in to provide greater scaffolding to help students decide what should go in the rest of the category boxes. This graphic organizer also has a concept bank. Students will fill in the category boxes with words or names from this randomly ordered list.

Directions: Below is a concept bank of names and battles from the chapter on the Civil War. Classify the vocabulary terms by arranging them into logical groups. Be prepared to show the logic behind your thinking.

Concept Bank:

General William T. Sherman
Battle of Fredericksburg
The Union
General Thomas J. "Stonewall" Jackson
General Pierre Beauregard
Battle of Vicksburg
Battle of Antietam

General Ulysses S. Grant
Battle of Gettysburg
Second Battle of Bull Run
General Robert E. Lee
General George B. McClellan
Battle of Chancellorsville
The Confederate States of America

Answer Key:

The following categories are logical groupings. However, students may vary these somewhat. For example, students may classify generals under battles in which they fought as acceptable categories.

The Confederate States of America

Generals:
  General Robert E. Lee
  General Pierre Beauregard
  General Thomas J. "Stonewall" Jackson

Battles Won by the Confederacy:
  Second Battle of Bull Run
  Battle of Fredericksburg
  Battle of Chancellorsville

The Union

Generals:
  General William T. Sherman
  General Ulysses S. Grant
  General George B. McClellan

Battles Won by the Union:
  Battle of Gettysburg
  Battle of Vicksburg
  Battle of Antietam

FIGURE 18–2   Example One of Open Sort for *The Story of America*

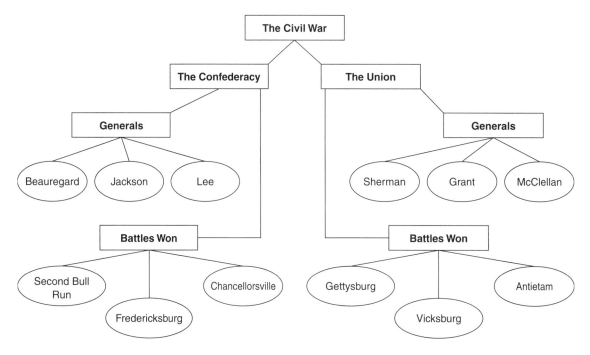

FIGURE 18–3   Example Two of Open Sort for *The Story of America*
Note: This open sort graphic organizer represents another way the teacher might require students to categorize the terms from the concept bank. The only requirement is that the students must be able to logically justify their arrangement of ideas in the hierarchical array. (See Strategy 14, Thinking Tree, pages 46–48.)

part of the closed sort and requires students to complete the remainder from the concept bank.

3. In the open sort for *The Story of America,* only the vocabulary list is provided. Students may group the words under logical headings as in Figure 18–2, or they many create a graphic organizer to visually represent the relationships among the concepts as in Figure 18–3.

4. Both closed and open sorts have an added advantage in developing reading comprehension in that they help students understand main idea-detail relationships, an essential component of hierarchical order.

FURTHER READING

Graves, M., Juel, C., & Graves, B. (1998). *Teaching reading in the 21st century.* Needham Heights, MA: Allyn & Bacon.

Gunning, T. (2005). *Creating literacy instruction for all students* (5th ed.). Boston: Allyn & Bacon.

Johns, J., & Lenski, S. D. (2001). *Improving reading: Strategies and resources* (3rd ed.). Dubuque, IA: Kendall/Hunt.

Reutzel, D. R., & Cooter, R. (2000). *Teaching children to read: Putting the pieces together* (3rd ed.). Columbus, OH: Merrill.

Vacca, J. A. L., Vacca, R. T., & Gove, M. K. (2000). *Reading and learning to read* (4th ed.). New York: Addison Wesley Longman.

Vacca, R. T., & Vacca, J. A. L. (2005). *Content area reading: Literacy and learning across the curriculum* (8th ed.). Boston: Allyn & Bacon.

19 Concept Circles

$\widehat{EL}$ *Also beneficial when working with English learners*

Strategy at a Glance: *Grade Levels All*

When to Use	Grouping	Literature Type	Skill Areas
● before reading	● individual	○ narrative	○ word recognition
● during reading	● small group	● expository	● vocabulary
● after reading	● whole class		● comprehension
	○ center		○ writing

Purpose

To assist in the categorization and collection of information to show the connections among concepts and their meanings from an instructional unit of study

Literature Used

Gregg Keyboarding and Personal Applications, by Alan Lloyd and others

Communicating in Spanish, by Conrad Schmitt and Protase W. Woodford

When to Use

Before, during, and/or after reading

Description of Strategy

Concept circles rely on visual representation to display whole-part connections among ideas. The parts in a circle contain concepts that all relate to each other in some way. By placing certain concepts in a circle, students are then able to determine a category (name of the circle) that all of the terms would logically belong to. Students are given the category names for each of the circles and asked to use literature they have been reading to fill in the concepts that go into each circle, or students may be given the collection of terms already in the circles and then are asked to determine the category names of the circles. In other variations, students may be given the concepts, categories, and empty concept circles and asked to determine where each would fit, or students may have to provide circles for the vocabulary and be asked to determine their own logical concepts and categories. The teacher can choose how to use this strategy based on the amount of scaffolding needed by the learners.

⑧ Procedures for Use

1. The teacher selects a unit of study containing concepts that lend themselves to logical groupings as in the *Gregg Keyboarding and Personal Applications* series for an introductory computer course.

2. *Before* students read and study the information, the teacher should preteach some of the key terms. Attention also should be drawn to important words *during* the lesson to provide multiple exposures to the vocabulary.

3. The teacher should introduce the strategy of concept circles and explain how they work, why they are helpful, and when to use them. That is, giving learners a purpose and building background are crucial components for making the activity successful.

4. *After* the information from the text has been read and discussed, the teacher asks the students to complete the concept circles. If students are not familiar with the activity, it may be helpful to demonstrate it with an example or two through modeling and/or guided practice.

5. In the example for *Gregg Keyboarding and Personal Applications* shown in Figure 19–1, students must mark out the word that does not logically fit into each circle of four terms and must determine the name of the category for the remaining three. Although these concept circles all have four terms, for other lessons there might be only three while others might have five or more per circle. The key idea is that the related terms have a logical basis for belonging to a category. Otherwise, students will misunderstand the process of classifying and collecting.

6. Instead of circles, the teacher may use concept boxes. For scaffolding in the activity for *Gregg Keyboarding and Personal Applications,* the teacher has provided a concept bank of headings or category names from which students may select correct choices to label each circle. The example from the foreign language textbook, *Communicating in Spanish,* shown in Figure 19–2, applies the principles of concept circles to names for foods. In this instance, however, baskets take the place of circles or squares. An answer key accompanies the activity. (See Figure 19–3.)

Directions: Shade the word in each concept circle that does not logically belong. On the line below each circle, write the word or phrase from the concept bank of headings to describe what the remaining words in each circle have in common.

Answer Key:

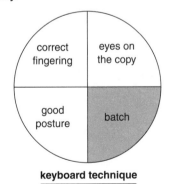

keyboard technique

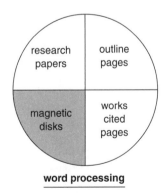

word processing

Concept Bank of Headings
storage
keyboard technique
computer classification
computer programs
word processing

FIGURE 19–1   Example for *Gregg Keyboarding and Personal Applications*

Comprando Comestibles

Label the baskets with the store categories and sort the vocabulary words into the appropriate baskets, based on the store in which each item is sold.

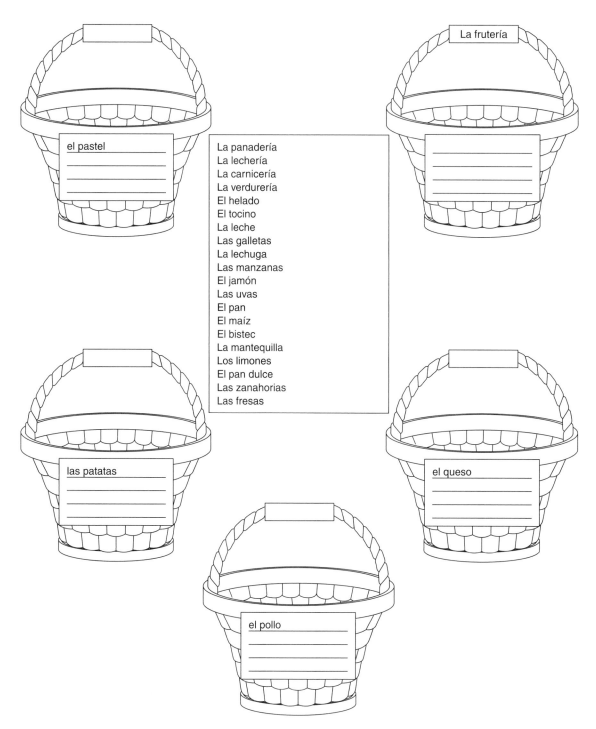

el pastel

La frutería

La panadería
La lechería
La carnicería
La verdurería
El helado
El tocino
La leche
Las galletas
La lechuga
Las manzanas
El jamón
Las uvas
El pan
El maíz
El bistec
La mantequilla
Los limones
El pan dulce
Las zanahorias
Las fresas

las patatas

el queso

el pollo

FIGURE 19–2   Example for *Communicating in Spanish*

Comprando Comestibles

Label the baskets with the store categories and sort the vocabulary words into the appropriate baskets, based on the store in which each item is sold.

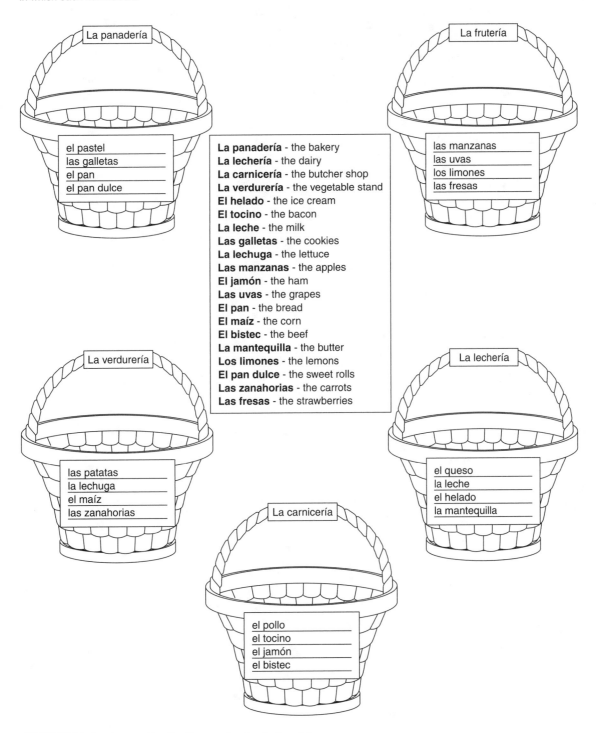

La panadería

el pastel
las galletas
el pan
el pan dulce

La frutería

las manzanas
las uvas
los limones
las fresas

La panadería - the bakery
La lechería - the dairy
La carnicería - the butcher shop
La verdurería - the vegetable stand
El helado - the ice cream
El tocino - the bacon
La leche - the milk
Las galletas - the cookies
La lechuga - the lettuce
Las manzanas - the apples
El jamón - the ham
Las uvas - the grapes
El pan - the bread
El maíz - the corn
El bistec - the beef
La mantequilla - the butter
Los limones - the lemons
El pan dulce - the sweet rolls
Las zanahorias - the carrots
Las fresas - the strawberries

La verdurería

las patatas
la lechuga
el maíz
las zanahorias

La lechería

el queso
la leche
el helado
la mantequilla

La carnicería

el pollo
el tocino
el jamón
el bistec

FIGURE 19–3 Answer Key for *Communicating in Spanish*

67

FURTHER READING

Gipe, J. P. (2006). *Multiple paths to literacy: Assessment and differentiated instruction for diverse learners, K–12* (6th ed.). Upper Saddle River, NJ: Merrill/Prentice Hall.

Johns, J., & Lenski, S. D. (2001). *Improving reading: Strategies and resources* (3rd ed.). Dubuque, IA: Kendall/Hunt.

Vacca, J. A. L., Vacca, R. T., & Gove, M. K. (2000). *Reading and learning to read* (4th ed.). New York: Addison Wesley Longman.

Vacca, R. T., & Vacca, J. A. L. (2005). *Content area reading: Literacy and learning across the curriculum* (8th ed.). Boston: Allyn & Bacon.

20 Analogies

(EL) *Also beneficial when working with English learners*

Strategy at a Glance: *Grade Levels 4–8*

When to Use	Grouping	Literature Type	Skill Areas
○ before reading	● individual	● narrative	○ word recognition
○ during reading	● small group	● expository	● vocabulary
● after reading	○ whole class		● comprehension
	○ center		○ writing

Purpose

To foster critical thinking and reinforcement of key vocabulary through the comparison of relationships in two pairs of words

Literature Used

American Government: Freedom, Rights, Responsibilities, by Vivian Bernstein

When to Use

After reading

Description of Strategy

Analogies develop critical thought through a comparison of like relationships. The teacher may construct numerous types of relationships for an activity to reinforce key terms through analogies. Common types of relationships include the following, which may serve as models for the teacher when he or she creates analogies:

1. Part to whole
   a is to *alphabet* as *toe* is to *foot*

2. Cause and effect
   prosperity is to *peace* as *poverty* is to *revolution*

3. Person to situation
   King George III is to *monarchy* as *Andrew Jackson* is to *democracy*

4. Antonym
   gluttony is to *fasting* as *war* is to *peace*

5. Synonym
   mob is to *rabble* as *elite* is to *nonesuch*

6. Geography
   ocean is to *Atlantic* as *continent* is to *Australia*

7. Person or character to task, country, birthplace, and so forth.
   Perseus is to *Medusa* as *St. George* is to *dragon*

8. Time or measurement
   second is to *minute* as *hour* is to *day*

9. Symbol
   light is to *hope* as *darkness* is to *despair*

10. Characteristic or trait
    Achilles is to *courage* as *Benedict Arnold* is to *treachery*

11. Degree
    piano is to *pianissimo* as *forte* is to *fortissimo*

For younger students, the teacher may want to familiarize them first with one or two types of analogies such as part to whole or synonyms. The follow-up vocabulary reinforcement strategy would concentrate on these relationships only. For older learners, a vocabulary reinforcement activity with analogies may contain a variety of different kinds of relationships for each pair of terms. Some analogies should have contrast; others, cause and effect; still others, part to whole; and so forth. A mixture will call for greater critical thinking than an exercise that has all of the analogies with only a single relationship. If students are not familiar with analogous relationships, the teacher should build background by modeling a few examples. Once students become more comfortable with analogies, they may take key terms and write their own.

Procedures for Use

1. Chapter 14 from *American Government: Freedom, Rights, Responsibilities,* by Vivian Bernstein, discusses political parties and is rich in concepts that require multiple exposures if students are to develop word power. The teacher should carefully examine the chapter to determine which terms need emphasis in support of learning outcomes. Some of these words should be introduced *before* reading, as others are emphasized *during* reading.

2. The activity with analogies comes *after* reading and helps learners get at the deeper dimensions of the connections among concepts as students problem-solve to determine relationships.

3. The example used in Figure 20–1 contains a sample analogy that the teacher models for students to help them become familiar with the nature of analogies. Scaffolding is further provided through a multiple-choice format for each item with four choices (a, b, c, d) listed. Students could be permitted to refer to their texts for additional help if key terms are unclear or have been forgotten.

4. The activity can be completed by students individually or cooperatively. If students work in collaborative groups, they receive the added reinforcement of hearing the words, saying the words, and reading the words.

Directions: Determine the relationship between the first pair of words, and then circle the letter of the word that similarly relates the second pair of words. These words are taken from Chapter 14 of *American Government: Freedom, Rights, Responsibilities.* You may refer to your book if necessary.

Example: CAR is to GAS as SAILBOAT is to:
        a. oar   b. wind   c. water   d. waves

You should have circled the letter b. Gas powers a car, and wind powers a sailboat.

1. GAMES are to BASEBALL as ELECTIONS are to:
   a. Constitution   b. political parties   c. United States   d. the first Tuesday in November

2. FEDERALIST is to REPUBLICAN as ANTIFEDERALIST is to:
   a. Congress   b. Libertarian   c. American Independent   d. Democrat

3. THIRD PARTY is to THEODORE ROOSEVELT as AMERICAN INDEPENDENT is to:
   a. George Wallace   b. George Washington   c. Lyndon B. Johnson   d. George Bush, Sr.

4. RACE is to RUNNER as ELECTION is to:
   a. voter   b. platform   c. candidate   d. polling place

5. BOOK is to WRITER as CONSTITUTION is to:
   a. framers   b. voters   c. candidates   d. citizens

6. FOOTBALL TEAM is to FAN as CANDIDATE is to:
   a. voter   b. citizen   c. election day   d. government

7. SOUP is to GROCERIES as VOTER is to:
   a. election day   b. member of Congress   c. eighteen years old   d. registration list

8. AUTOMOBILE is to DRIVER'S LICENSE as VOTING is to:
   a. citizenship   b. president   c. platform   d. political advertisement

9. EATING is to DINING ROOM as VOTING is to:
   a. platform   b. Republicans   c. Democrats   d. polling place

10. COLD is to ICE CREAM as FREE ELECTION is to:
   a. democracy   b. volunteer worker   c. nonvoter   d. Fourth of July

Key:

1. b	6. a
2. d	7. d
3. a	8. a
4. c	9. d
5. a	10. a

FIGURE 20–1   Example for *American Government: Freedom, Rights, Responsibilities*

FURTHER READING

Gunning, T. (2005). *Creating literacy instruction for all students* (5th ed.). Boston: Allyn & Bacon.

Harris, A. J., & Sipay, E. R. (1990). *How to increase reading ability: A guide to developmental and remedial methods* (9th ed.). New York: Longman.

Vacca, J. A. L., Vacca, R. T., & Gove, M. K. (2000). *Reading and learning to read* (4th ed.). New York: Addison Wesley Longman.

21

Frayer Model

(EL) *Also beneficial when working with English learners*

Strategy at a Glance: *Grade Levels All*

When to Use	Grouping	Literature Type	Skill Areas
● before reading	● individual	● narrative	○ word recognition
● during reading	● small group	● expository	● vocabulary
● after reading	● whole class		● comprehension
	○ center		○ writing

Purpose

To develop the meaning of vocabulary words through analysis of essential and nonessential properties and through examples and nonexamples

Literature Used

The Librarian who Measured the Earth, by Kathryn Lasky

When to Use

Before, during, or after reading

Description of Strategy

The Frayer Model helps students understand the deeper dimensions of a word's meaning and may be used to study a difficult vocabulary concept either *before*, *during*, or *after* reading. *Before* reading, teachers use the Frayer Model to introduce or preview a new vocabulary word. *During* reading, the strategy may serve as part of an on-the-spot mini-lesson for a difficult concept students encounter. *After* reading, the strategy may provide additional exposure to reinforce comprehension of a concept. The technique gives learners a structure, usually in the form of a four-square activity, to organize information about a word into blocks containing attributes, non-attributes, examples, and non-examples. In the center of the four squares is a circle containing the word and a definition. The purpose of the Frayer Model is to aid understanding through knowledge of what something is as well as through knowledge of what it is not.

8 Procedures for Use

1. On a worksheet, chart paper, overhead projector, or board, the teacher provides learners with a four-square diagram which they will use to organize information about a difficult vocabulary concept. Figure 21–1 shows one way a four square might look. Starting clockwise from the upper left box, each box is labeled as follows: essential features, non-essential features, non-examples, and examples.

2. In the center of the four-square diagram is a circle (or oval). This should be large enough so that students have room to write the word and its definition. (See Figure 21–1.) The definition may be recorded before or after students have discussed and decided upon which relevant and irrelevant features and examples go in the four boxes. The definition may be from a dictionary or in the students' own words.

3. The teacher explains the purpose of the four square and should scaffold the activity through initial modeling followed by guided practice and then independent practice for students as they complete the boxes. Students may work individually, in pairs, in small groups, or as a whole class. As learners become accustomed to the process, they can work more independently.

4. Figure 21–2 illustrates a completed four square for the concept "circumference" from Kathryn Lasky's *The Librarian Who Measured the Earth,* a picture book biography of the ancient Greek mathematician Erastothenes, who determined the circumference of the earth through logical analysis. This text might serve as helpful supplementary reading to the study of geometry in math.

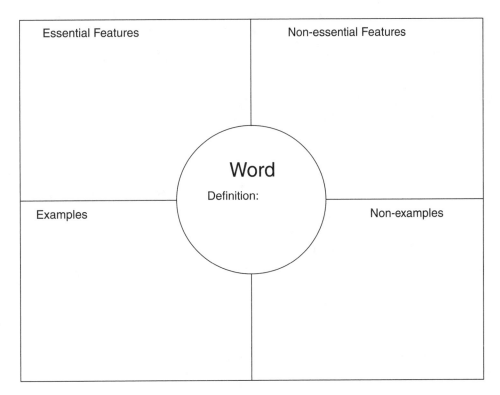

FIGURE 21–1   Example of a Four Square for the Frayer Model

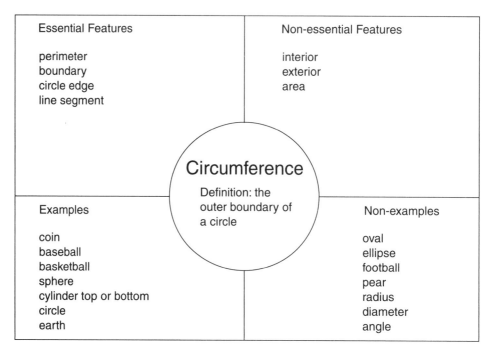

FIGURE 21–2   Example of a Completed Four Square for *The Librarian Who Measured the Earth*

FURTHER READING

Billmeyer, R., & Barton, M. L. (2002). *Teaching reading in the content areas: If not me, then who?* (2nd ed.). Aurora, CO: Mid-Continent Research for Education and Learning.

Frayer, D. A., Frederick, W. C., & Klausmeier, H. J. (1969). *A schema for testing the level of concept mastery.* Technical Report No. 16. Madison, WI: University of Wisconsin Research and Development Center for Cognitive Learning.

Gipe, J. P. (2006). *Multiple paths to literacy: Assessment and differentiated instruction for diverse learners, K–12* (6th ed.). Upper Saddle River, NJ: Merrill/Prentice Hall.

Tierney, R. J., & Readence, J. E. (2000). *Reading strategies and practices: A compendium* (5th ed.). Boston: Allyn & Bacon.

PART IV

Comprehension Strategies

22 Chaining for Time Order or for One-to-One Cause and Effect and/or Problem Solution

(EL) *Also beneficial when working with English learners*

Strategy at a Glance: *Grade Levels All*

When to Use	Grouping	Literature Type	Skill Areas
○ before reading	○ individual	● narrative	○ word recognition
● during reading	● small group	● expository	● vocabulary
● after reading	● whole class		● comprehension
	○ center		● writing

Purpose

To help students understand a chronological sequence, a cause and effect series, or a problem-solution pattern of organization from a narrative or expository passage

Literature Used

If You Give a Mouse a Cookie, by Laura Numeroff

Abe Lincoln's Hat, by Martha Brenner

When to Use

During or after reading

Description of Strategy

Chaining provides a graphic representation to students to aid them in understanding chronological sequence or in comprehending how one cause may lead to one effect, which may then become a cause leading to another effect, and so on in narrative or informational text. The same idea also applies to problem-solution organizational patterns.

Procedures for Use

1. The teacher and students share a book that has sequential, or chronological, order, cause and effect relationships, or both, as is the case with *If You Give a Mouse a Cookie*.

2. The teacher and students discuss the meanings of cause and effect or of chronological order *before* reading. The discussion should apply these concepts of reading comprehension to experiences familiar to learners in order to activate their background knowledge. The teacher might say, "I was hungry" and explain that this effect caused her to get something to eat. The students then might offer some additional familiar examples of cause and effect. The discussion should also set a purpose for learners so that, when they read or listen to the text, they will know to pay attention to time sequence and/or cause and effect.

3. The teacher reads *If You Give a Mouse a Cookie* and uses a prepared chart on chronological order, cause and effect, or both. Parts of the sequence or some of the causes and effects are provided on the chart. (See the example for *If You Give a Mouse a Cookie* in Figure 22–1.) Students work with the teacher or independently to complete the chart. Some learners will need more teacher guidance than others. A picture, a word, a phrase, an entire sentence, or a combination of these may be

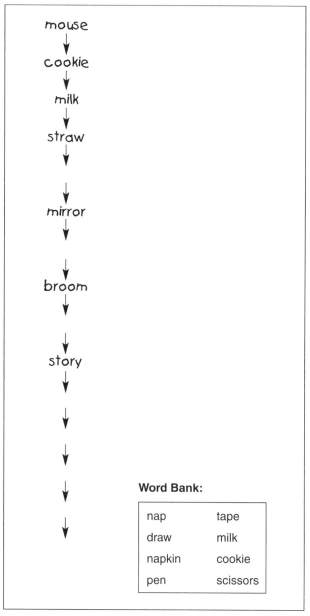

FIGURE 22–1   Example for *If You Give a Mouse a Cookie*

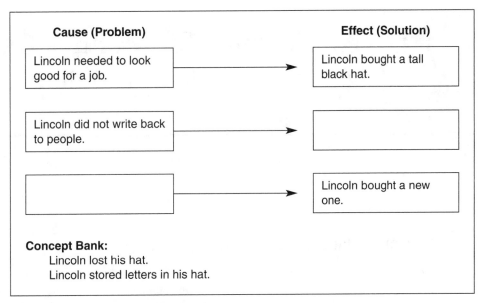

FIGURE 22–2   Example for *Abe Lincoln's Hat*

used depending on the needs of the class. In the example, single words or prompts are given. The student says a sentence using the word that shows cause-effect relationships. For example, a class member might say, "Because the **mouse** was hungry, he ate a **cookie**."

4. Once the chart is completed, the teacher and students should discuss it and read it. The teacher may read it *aloud* to the students and then invite them to read *along* together, following the teacher's lead.

5. As a final step, students read the completed chart *alone*.

6. For less able learners, a concept bank of missing portions of the sequence or of causes and effects may be helpful for them to make selections to go in the chart. (This scaffolding technique is used in the example for *If You Give a Mouse a Cookie*.)

7. The example for *Abe Lincoln's Hat* in Figure 22–2 shows chains for a text in which one cause (or problem) exists for one effect (or solution). Students must determine these *during* or *after* reading. A concept bank provides additional scaffolding, if needed. Teacher modeling and guidance will be essential for some learners.

FURTHER READING

Cooper, J. D. (2000). *Literacy: Helping children construct meaning* (4th ed.). Boston: Houghton Mifflin.

Gunning, T. (2005). *Creating literacy instruction for all students* (5th ed.). Boston: Allyn & Bacon.

Harris, A. J., & Sipay, E. R. (1990). *How to increase reading ability: A guide to developmental and remedial methods* (9th ed.). New York: Longman.

Johns, J., & Lenski, S. D. (2001). *Improving reading: Strategies and resources* (3rd ed.). Dubuque, IA: Kendall/Hunt.

Reutzel, D. R., & Cooter, R. (2000). *Teaching children to read: Putting the pieces together* (3rd ed.). Columbus, OH: Merrill.

Tompkins, G. E. (2005). *Language arts: Patterns of practice* (6th ed.). Upper Saddle River, NJ: Merrill/Prentice Hall.

Vacca, R. T., & Vacca, J. A. L. (2005). *Content area reading: Literacy and learning across the curriculum* (8th ed.). Boston: Allyn & Bacon.

23

Chaining for Multiple Causes and Effects or Problem Solutions

 Also beneficial when working with English learners

Strategy at a Glance: *Grade Levels 4–8*

When to Use	Grouping	Literature Type	Skill Areas
○ before reading	○ individual	● narrative	○ word recognition
● during reading	● small group	● expository	● vocabulary
● after reading	● whole class		● comprehension
	○ center		● writing

Purpose

To determine multiple causes having one effect or effects, multiple effects having one cause or causes, multiple solutions having a single problem or problems, or multiple problems having a single solution or solutions

Literature Used

Farmer Duck, by Martin Waddell

When to Use

During or after reading

Description of Strategy

Cause and effect chains can help readers understand the reason(s) for a consequence or for several consequences. The effects are recorded on a chart as a visual aid for learners to see the causes and effects (or problems and solutions) in narrative or expository text.

Procedures for Use

1. *Before* reading, the teacher prepares a cause and effect chart or problem-solution chart similar to the example for *Farmer Duck* in Figure 23–1. The teacher then decides which causes and effects to omit for students to fill in later either *during* or *after* reading. The example for *Farmer Duck* shows the completed chart. As much may be omitted or filled in as the teacher deems appropriate for the learners with whom it will be used.

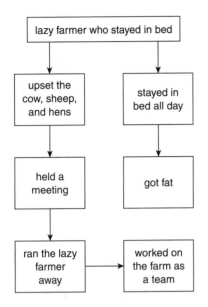
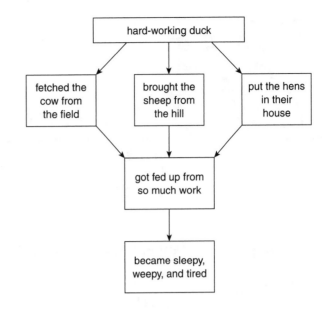

FIGURE 23–1   Example for *Farmer Duck*

2. *After* reading, the teacher models the procedure by discussing how one event results in one or several consequences, which may then become a cause or causes for other events.

3. Students will continue the procedure with teacher guidance and further modeling or thinking aloud for the remaining causes and effects.

4. A concept bank of causes and effects or problems and solutions is a helpful aid for less able learners.

FURTHER READING

Harris, A. J., & Sipay, E. R. (1990). *How to increase reading ability: A guide to developmental and remedial methods* (9th ed.). New York: Longman.

Reutzel, D. R., & Cooter, R. (2000). *Teaching children to read: Putting the pieces together* (3rd ed.). Columbus, OH: Merrill.

Tompkins, G. E. (2005). *Language arts: Patterns of practice* (6th ed.). Upper Saddle River, NJ: Merrill/Prentice Hall.

Vacca, R. T., & Vacca, J. A. L. (2005). *Content area reading: Literacy and learning across the curriculum* (8th ed.). Boston: Allyn & Bacon.

24 Plot-Relationship Chart

EL *Also beneficial when working with English learners*

Strategy at a Glance: *Grade Levels All*

When to Use	Grouping	Literature Type	Skill Areas
◯ before reading	◯ individual	● narrative	◯ word recognition
◯ during reading	● small group	● expository	● vocabulary
● after reading	● whole class		● comprehension
	◯ center		● writing

Purpose

To aid in the understanding and summarizing of story grammar elements, particularly main character and problem/resolution attempts in narrative material

Literature Used

"The Gambling Ghost," in *Gaelic Ghosts*, by Sorche Nic Leodhas, pages 39–46

When to Use

After reading

Description of Strategy

A plot-relationship chart is a graphic organizer consisting of four columns. Each of the columns concerns the main character, a problem that the character wants to resolve, the opposing force that gets in the way of the resolution, and how the problem is resolved. Usually the columns are labeled as follows: SOMEBODY, WANTED, BUT, and SO. SOMEBODY corresponds to the main character, or protagonist, of the story; WANTED, to the goal the protagonist wishes to accomplish or the problem to be resolved; BUT, to the antagonist, or force(s) in opposition to the main character; and SO, to how the goal is achieved or the problem is resolved. The teacher may change these column headings to better suit the capabilities of students or the age-appropriateness of the story. For instance, for older learners, the word "protagonist" may be substituted for "somebody." A plot-relationship chart also may be used to summarize or compare and contrast the plots of several different stories. This adaptation occurs by adding rows for other stories read.

Somebody	Wanted	But	So
Lad	money in order to gamble	He had taken everyone's money and did not have anyone to gamble with.	Lad gambled with a ghost who wanted to win his soul. Lad got scared, stopped gambling, got a job, and saved money.

Plot Summary Sentence(s):

_____

_____

FIGURE 24–1   Example for "The Gambling Ghost"

Procedures for Use

1. Students read independently or with teacher guidance "The Gambling Ghost" from the book *Gaelic Ghosts*.

2. The teacher and students discuss the story in terms of the chart so that students will have an idea of what the components (SOMEBODY, WANTED, BUT, SO) of the plot-relationship chart entail. (See Figure 24–1.)

3. The students fill in the chart using their own words. Teacher guidance may be necessary for some learners during this step.

4. After the chart is completed, students can summarize the plot in one or two written sentences.

5. For some learners, the chart may need to be explained *before* the story is read so that a clear purpose for reading and strategy background are established.

FURTHER READING

Cunningham, P., & Allington, R. (1994). *Classrooms that work*. New York: HarperCollins.

Gipe, J. P. (2006). *Multiple paths to literacy: Assessment and differentiated instruction for diverse learners, K–12* (6th ed.) Upper Saddle River, NJ: Merrill/Prentice Hall.

Harris, A. J., & Sipay, E. R. (1990). *How to increase reading ability: A guide to developmental and remedial methods* (9th ed.). New York: Longman.

Johns, J., & Lenski, S. D. (2001). *Improving reading: Strategies and resources* (3rd ed.). Dubuque, IA: Kendall/Hunt.

Norton, D. E., & Norton, S. E. (2003). *Through the eyes of a child: An introduction to children's literature* (6th ed.). Upper Saddle River, NJ: Merrill/Prentice Hall.

Tierney, R. J., & Readence, J. E. (2000). *Reading strategies and practices: A compendium* (5th ed.). Boston: Allyn & Bacon.

Tompkins, G. E. (2005). *Language arts: Patterns of practice* (6th ed.). Upper Saddle River, NJ: Merrill/Prentice Hall.

25 Story Pyramid

 Also beneficial when working with English learners

Strategy at a Glance: *Grade Levels All*

When to Use	Grouping	Literature Type	Skill Areas
○ before reading	● individual	● narrative	● word recognition
○ during reading	● small group	● expository	● vocabulary
● after reading	● whole class		● comprehension
	○ center		● writing

Purpose

To improve the ability to understand and describe such parts of story grammar in narrative writing as setting, characterization, problem-resolution, other major plot events, and theme

Literature Used

Monster Mama, by Liz Rosenberg

The Girl Who Loved Wild Horses, by Paul Goble

When to Use

After reading

Description of Strategy

The story pyramid is a comprehension activity that is often arranged in the shape of a tri-angle or pyramid. The first line consists of one blank, while the second line has two blanks, and so forth. Each line has a required pattern that students read and then fill in the blank(s) with information from the story to fulfill the stipulations. The following is a sample of what each line's requirement may be:

1. Name of the main character
2. Two words describing the main character
3. Three words describing the setting
4. Four words stating the problem
5. Five words describing the first event
6. Six words describing the second event
7. Seven words describing the third event
8. Eight words stating the solution

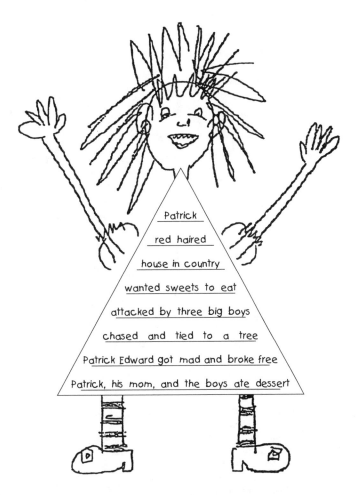

Patrick

red haired

house in country

wanted sweets to eat

attacked by three big boys

chased and tied to a tree

Patrick Edward got mad and broke free

Patrick, his mom, and the boys ate dessert

Theme or moral: _____

_____

_____

Story Pyramid

1. Name of the main character
2. Two words describing the main character
3. Three words describing the setting
4. Four words stating the problem
5. Five words describing the first event
6. Six words describing the second event
7. Seven words describing the third event
8. Eight words stating the solution
9. (*Optional*) A sentence stating the theme or moral of the story

FIGURE 25–1   Example for *Monster Mama*

Alterations in the requirements for each line are welcome since these may be changed to fit a particular story or the needs of different students. Some stories may need more than eight pyramid parts because these stories contain more than three major events. Another alteration is to have students write the theme or moral of the story in a complete sentence as the last line of the triangle. A further variation that might help in the facilitation of this activity is to add graphics around or to substitute them for the triangle. For example, the graphic for *Monster Mama* has students complete a triangular body of the mother in the story. (See Figure 25–1.) The graphic for a story pyramid of Paul Goble's *The Girl Who Loved Wild Horses* is done in the shape of a teepee since the book is about a legend of

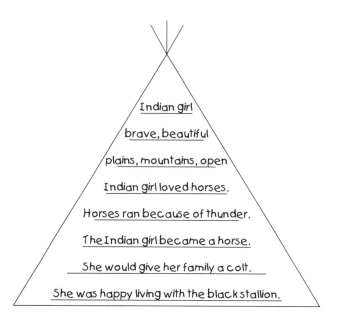

Theme or moral: _____

_____

Story Pyramid

1. Name of the main character
2. Two words describing the main character
3. Three words describing the setting
4. Four words stating the problem
5. Five words describing the first event
6. Six words describing the second event
7. Seven words describing the third event
8. Eight words stating the solution
9. (*Optional*) A sentence stating the theme or moral of the story

FIGURE 25–2   Example for *The Girl Who Loved Wild Horses*

the Plains Indians. (See Figure 25–2.) The strategy not only fosters understanding of the story elements but also promotes competence in summarizing narrative text.

Procedures for Use

1. Any narrative may be used, whether poetry or prose.

2. Based on the students' needs, the teacher decides the reading mode; for *Monster Mama* and *The Girl Who Loved Wild Horses,* the selected mode is read *aloud, along,* and *alone* so as to give the necessary scaffolding for learners to aid in sight word recognition through repeated readings. This procedure facilitates automaticity in pronouncing words.

3. Students listen carefully as the teacher reads *aloud.*

4. Students read the text *along* with the teacher and then, as a final step, read *alone.*

5. The teacher describes and explains the story pyramid and sets the purpose for using it.

6. If readers have not previously worked with story pyramids, the teacher may want to guide them in arriving at the answers. For example, the first line of the pyramid for *Monster Mama* would be "Patrick," the name of the little boy in the story.

7. The students complete the pyramid by filling in the blanks. The teacher provides instructional guidance as necessary. The information on the pyramid may be used to model a retelling of the story.

FURTHER READING

Harris, A. J., & Sipay, E. R. (1990). *How to increase reading ability: A guide to developmental and remedial methods* (9th ed.). New York: Longman.

Johns, J., & Lenski, S. D. (2001). *Improving reading: Strategies and resources* (3rd ed.). Dubuque, IA: Kendall/Hunt.

Norton, D. E., & Norton, S. E. (2003). *Through the eyes of a child: An introduction to children's literature* (6th ed.). Upper Saddle River, NJ: Merrill/Prentice Hall.

Tierney, R. J., & Readence, J. E. (2000). *Reading strategies and practices: A compendium* (5th ed.). Boston: Allyn & Bacon.

Tompkins, G. E. (2005). *Language arts: Patterns of practice* (6th ed.). Upper Saddle River, NJ: Merrill/Prentice Hall.

26 Three-Dimensional Text Pyramid

(EL) *Also beneficial when working with English learners*

Strategy at a Glance: *Grade Levels All*

When to Use	Grouping	Literature Type	Skill Areas
○ before reading	● individual	● narrative	○ word recognition
○ during reading	● small group	● expository	● vocabulary
● after reading	● whole class		● comprehension
	● center		● writing

Purpose

To develop facility in describing a main setting or character from narrative text or a key topic from expository text

Literature Used

Lizards and Dragons, by Lionel Bender

When to Use

After reading

Description of Strategy

The three-dimensional text pyramid uses questions to help students describe in detail important components of reading comprehension like setting, character, or main idea. The strategy works with narrative or expository passages in which recall of detail is important. Generally, the teacher poses six questions (more may be asked) to which students write answers. These may be recorded by the teacher, if necessary.

For each question, students respond with the same number of words that correspond to the particular number of the question so that a one-word response is given for question one, two words for question two, and so forth. Responses are written on cardboard boxes—with one word put in each box for a total of 21. (Instead of writing directly on the boxes, students may record responses on self adhesive notes to attach to the boxes later.) Thus, the answer for question one is one word recorded on one box, while the answer for question two is two words recorded on two boxes. This procedure continues through question six, for which six words are written on six boxes. Once all the questions are answered, students should stack their boxes in the reverse order in which the questions were asked. The six boxes for question six become the base, those for question five the next layer, those for question four the next, and so on. This process continues until the pyramid is built with the last box for question one being the apex.

A good way to familiarize learners not acquainted with a three-dimensional text pyramid is to have them build a pyramid about themselves before making one based on a reading passage. The following are hypothetical questions to use for an initial pyramid:

1. What is your name?
2. What are two words that describe you?
3. What are three words describing where you live?
4. Who are four of your friends?
5. What are five features that all of them have that make you like them?
6. What are six of the favorite things you like to do with your friends (foods to eat, places to go, and so on)?

As item six shows, the teacher may alter the questions as necessary.

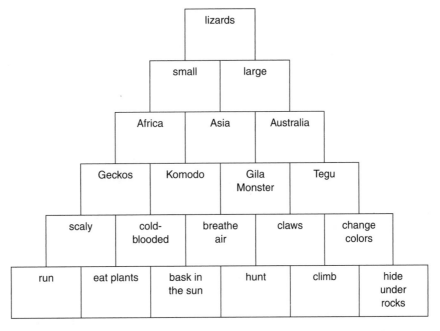

Questions for Three-Dimensional Text Pyramid

1. What is the main topic or subject of the reading passage? (The answer may be one word or several).
2. What are two words that describe the main topic in question one?
3. Where are three continents where the main topic in question one is found?
4. What are four examples of the main topic in question one?
5. What are five characteristics that may describe the main topic in question one or the four examples in question four?
6. What are six words or phrases that may describe what the four examples in question four do?

FIGURE 26–1 Example for *Lizards and Dragons*

𝒞 **Procedures for Use**

1. Any reading source, whether narrative or expository, is appropriate as long as it allows learners an opportunity to recall descriptive details. In this case, *Lizards and Dragons,* by Lionel Bender, contains many details about the topic "lizards."

2. Depending upon students' needs, the teacher uses an appropriate reading mode. This might be independent or guided.

3. Once the passage on lizards has been read, students answer questions requiring them to recall important details about the topic. The teacher should connect the activity to the previous pyramid that learners completed about themselves, if they are not familiar with the strategy of three-dimensional text pyramids.

4. Questions to ask about the passage are listed in the example for *Lizards and Dragons* in Figure 26–1. Alterations to these are, of course, welcome, for this text or others, depending upon the type of passage, the teacher's purpose, and the readers' needs.

FURTHER READING

Harris, A. J., & Sipay, E. R. (1990). *How to increase reading ability: A guide to developmental and remedial methods* (9th ed.). New York: Longman.

Johns, J., & Lenski, S. D. (2001). *Improving reading: Strategies and resources* (3rd ed.). Dubuque, IA: Kendall/Hunt.

Norton, D. E., & Norton, S. E. (2003). *Through the eyes of a child: An introduction to children's literature* (6th ed.). Upper Saddle River, NJ: Merrill/Prentice Hall.

Tierney, R. J., & Readence, J. E. (2000). *Reading strategies and practices: A compendium* (5th ed.). Boston: Allyn & Bacon.

Tompkins, G. E. (2005). *Language arts: Patterns of practice* (6th ed.). Upper Saddle River, NJ: Merrill/Prentice Hall.

27 Picture Walk or Text Walk

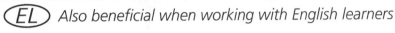 Also beneficial when working with English learners

Strategy at a Glance: *Grade Levels All*

When to Use	Grouping	Literature Type	Skill Areas
● before reading	○ individual	● narrative	○ word recognition
○ during reading	● small group	● expository	● vocabulary
○ after reading	● whole class		● comprehension
	○ center		○ writing

Purpose

To improve comprehension by activating the reader's background of experience or by developing additional knowledge about the content, organization, and vocabulary of narrative or expository text

Literature Used

The Story of Ferdinand, by Munro Leaf

When to Use

Before reading

Description of Strategy

Before reading occurs, the teacher previews and discusses the passage and asks questions about any illustrations, photographs, charts, or other graphics, whether the text is narrative or expository. In this way, students are provided with an overview of important ideas, organizational structure, and key vocabulary words. Before doing the picture or text walk, the teacher should read through the passage that will be used and note important concepts and vocabulary to emphasize. During this phase, the teacher should also jot down any questions that will activate a reader's background knowledge and develop an understanding of the reading material. A good idea is to include both efferent and aesthetic questions or comments during the picture or text walk. Efferent questions or comments will draw attention to important content ideas or to literacy competencies relevant in the passage such as main ideas, details, or significant vocabulary words, whereas aesthetic questions or comments will engage students on a personal level so that motivation for reading is likely increased. Usually, the term "picture walk" is preferred when the strategy is used for narrative text in picture books. The term "text walk" is used when the passage is from content-area materials or expository writing. In many instances, the teacher will want to do a picture or text walk on only a portion of the reading material, particularly when storybooks or narrative texts have unusual happenings or surprise endings that should not be revealed beforehand to learners.

Procedures for Use

1. The teacher should read *The Story of Ferdinand* ahead of time to determine the key components of the storyline and to decide which illustrations best reflect those ideas in order to preview and discuss them with students.

2. The teacher may begin the picture walk by stating the title and showing students the cover of the book, featuring Ferdinand the Bull. Efferent questions or prompts may be asked such as "What is Ferdinand doing? Where is he standing? What does it look like he is smelling?" The white daisies may be emphasized since Ferdinand's favorite activity is to sit quietly under the cork tree and smell the flowers.

3. The teacher may want to discuss the inside cover of the book to show students how the people of Madrid mistakenly think that Ferdinand is a fierce bull. The Spanish phrase "EL TORO FEROZ FERDINANDO" on the advertisement for the bullfight may be translated for students to point out the contrast between the people's perception of Ferdinand as a large, fierce bull and his true gentle nature. Some examples of aesthetic questions might include "Have you ever seen a bull? Did you think it looked ferocious? Do you think Ferdinand looks ferocious in the poster on the inside front cover? Would you want to fight a bull that looked like this picture of Ferdinand? How about here in the picture showing Ferdinand as a young bull sitting under the cork tree where he watches the other young bulls run and butt their heads together?"

4. To aid with understanding difficult vocabulary words, the teacher may want to preview some of the illustrations of the participants in the bullfight in Madrid by emphasizing pictures of the banderilleros, the picadores, and the matador.

5. In a picture walk with this text, it is likely that the teacher will not want to showcase the illustrations and story in the last few pages since Ferdinand surprises the bullfighters and the people in the arena by sitting down and refusing to fight because he smells flowers in the hair of the lovely ladies in attendance. However, the teacher may ask students to make predictions about this portion of the plot so that, when the story is read later, the students may verify their hypotheses.

6. Students can now read the story in whatever mode is appropriate, whether shared, guided, cooperative, or independent. Alternatively, the teacher may read the story aloud as students listen.

FURTHER READING

Cooper, J. D. (2000). *Literacy: Helping children construct meaning* (4th ed.). Boston: Houghton Mifflin.

Gunning, T. (2005). *Creating literacy instruction for all students* (5th ed.). Boston: Allyn & Bacon.

Johns, J., & Lenski, S. D. (2001). *Improving reading: Strategies and resources* (3rd ed.). Dubuque, IA: Kendall/Hunt.

Reutzel, D. R., & Cooter, R. (2000). *Teaching children to read: Putting the pieces together* (3rd ed.). Columbus, OH: Merrill.

Tompkins, G. E. (2005). *Language arts: Patterns of practice* (6th ed.). Upper Saddle River, NJ: Merrill/Prentice Hall.

28 Readers' Theater

 Also beneficial when working with English learners

Strategy at a Glance: *Grade Levels All*

When to Use	Grouping	Literature Type	Skill Areas
○ before reading	○ individual	● narrative	○ word recognition
○ during reading	● small group	○ expository	● vocabulary
● after reading	● whole class		● comprehension
	○ center		● writing

Purpose

To enhance listening, speaking, reading, and writing through creative interpretations of narrative text

Literature Used

"The Story of the Three Little Pigs," from Joseph Jacobs' *English Fairy Tales*

When to Use

After reading

Description of Strategy

Readers' theater is a strategy that fosters comprehension through creative interpretations of narratives by engaging students in role-playing stories, poems, or songs. Although the strategy focuses on the oral aspect of the language arts by allowing students to bring the characters to life through their voices, other language arts such as listening and reading are also integrated. Once learners are accustomed to the technique of readers' theater, they may create scripts and thereby develop facility with writing. When presenting readers' theater, students do not memorize lines; instead, as the name says, they *read* from a script after they have had time to practice good oral interpretation skills.

Procedures for Use

1. *After* the teacher and students have studied a narrative text, whether picture book, novel, poem, or song, the teacher may decide that the text is appropriate for readers' theater as an enrichment activity that develops literary appreciation as well as

language arts competencies. The key consideration is that the passage have enough dialogue for division into different character roles for students to read.

2. The teacher and students divide the text into parts. Students should have a copy of the passage to mark. More advanced students may divide the text on their own for presentation.

3. With the teacher's assistance, students identify and list all the characters. Their speaking parts are then marked and narrative tags such as "he said" or "she said" are omitted, leaving only the dialogue. Students are assigned these parts to read. A single character may have more than one reader. In fact, two or more students can simultaneously read one character's dialogue. The point is that all members of the class participate either as characters or narrators. In point of fact, essential narrative sections may be retained for oral reading by one narrator, by several separate narrators taking turns, or by a group of narrators functioning as a chorus.

4. Theatrical interpolations may be added such as a scream, a whistle, or an animal sound like a dog's bark. In "The Story of the Three Little Pigs," a theatrical interpolation might be the knocking by the wolf on the door of one of the pigs. A student can make this sound effect when the script requires it.

5. As steps 3 and 4 indicate, an essential key to readers' theater is that each student is involved. No one is left out. As each student chooses or is assigned to a role, these are marked on the passage with **N** for narrator or with a character's name. Sometimes different colored pens for each part work well. For interpolations, students make notes as to the time they are to create a sound effect.

6. The teacher should allow students time to prepare and rehearse the play before it is presented so that they may hone good oral interpretation skills with literature.

7. Readers' theater works also well for small collaborative groups within a class to present different stories studied. In a unit on folklore, one group might present "The Story of the Three Little Pigs"; another, "Henny Penny"; and another, "Goldilocks and the Three Bears." As students prepare and rehearse their stories, they develop skills in cooperative problem solving.

FURTHER READING

Cooper, J. D. (2000). *Literacy: Helping children construct meaning* (4th ed.). Boston: Houghton Mifflin.

Gunning, T. (2005). *Creating literacy instruction for all students* (5th ed.). Boston: Allyn & Bacon.

Johns, J., & Lenski, S. D. (2001). *Improving reading: Strategies and resources* (3rd ed.). Dubuque, IA: Kendall/Hunt.

Reutzel, D. R., & Cooter, R. (2000). *Teaching children to read: Putting the pieces together* (3rd ed.). Columbus, OH: Merrill.

Ruddell, R. B., & Ruddell, M. R. (1995). *Teaching children to read and write: Becoming an influential teacher*. Boston: Allyn & Bacon.

Tierney, R. J., & Readence, J. E. (2000). *Reading strategies and practices: A compendium* (5th ed.). Boston: Allyn & Bacon.

Tompkins, G. E. (2005). *Language arts: Patterns of practice* (6th ed.). Upper Saddle River, NJ: Merrill/Prentice Hall.

Wood, K. D., & Dickinson, T. S. (Eds.). (2000). *Promoting literacy in grades 4–9: A handbook for teachers and administrators*. Boston: Allyn & Bacon.

29 Modified Pocket Chart

EL Also beneficial when working with English learners

Strategy at a Glance: *Grade Levels 1–6*

When to Use	Grouping	Literature Type	Skill Areas
○ before reading	○ individual	● narrative	● word recognition
○ during reading	● small group	● expository	● vocabulary
● after reading	● whole class		● comprehension
	○ center		● writing

Purpose

To reinforce knowledge of story sequence

Literature Used

Just Me and My Dad, by Mercer Mayer

When to Use

After reading

Description of Strategy

A pocket chart, typically constructed from cloth, plastic, or heavy paper, is most often used for the development of word recognition. (See pages 9–10.) However, the version discussed here is a simple piece of blue posterboard with clothespins attached to it by hot glue. (See Figure 29–1.) Its purpose is to help students focus on the sequence of events. *After* a story is read, the teacher asks students to tell what happened in the story from beginning to end. While they are recalling the events, the teacher records the retelling or its significant parts. The teacher then rewrites individual events on sentence strips, all of equal length. This same procedure works also for language experience stories that students dictate to the teacher. (See pages 19–21.)

Once the sentence strips are made, the teacher arranges them so that they are out of order. Students must place the strips on the pocket chart in the same order that the story took place. This pocket chart strategy allows physical manipulation of the story events as students learn the correct sequence. The sentence strips should be of equal length so that the size of the strip will not act as an extraneous decoding clue for learners.

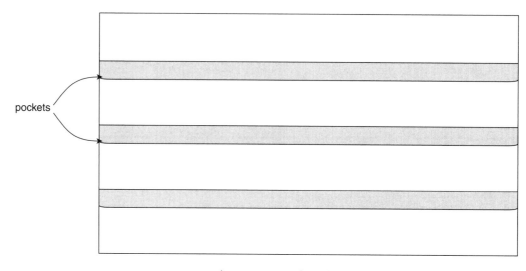

cards or sentence strips to insert into pockets

The	little	critter

alternate:

posterboard

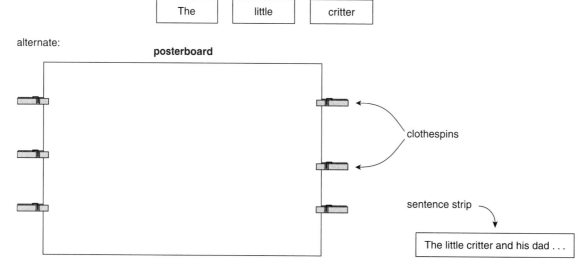

clothespins

sentence strip

The little critter and his dad . . .

The reader attaches sentences in order to the posterboard using the clothespins.

FIGURE 29–1   Pocket Chart

Procedures for Use

1. For *Just Me and My Dad,* the teacher reads the story *aloud* as students are directed to listen carefully to recall major events from the story in the order in which they occur. Other modes of reading may be used, depending on the learners, but the purpose should be the same as that given.

2. Once students hear the story, the teacher asks them to recall major events. The teacher records these on sentence strips of uniform size. Students observe the teacher recording events and listen as these are read *aloud.*

3. For less able learners, the teacher may scaffold the activity by asking questions to help students recall the sequence of events. Possible questions and responses for *Just Me and My Dad* are:

   Question: Where were the little critter and his dad at the beginning of the story?

   Response: The little critter and his dad were at home.

Question: Where did the little critter and his dad go next?

Response: They went to a campsite.

Question: Once they found a suitable campsite, what did the little critter and his dad do?

Response: They went to the river to fish.

Question: After they finished fishing, what did the two do next?

Response: They went back to their campsite.

During these prompts, the teacher may want to engage in purposeful rereading of relevant parts of the book so that students listen again in order to formulate answers. If students have their own copies of the text, the teacher may direct them to reread certain passages to determine the correct event for a question.

4. After the teacher has written the events on sentence strips, these can be randomly ordered for students to place in correct sequence on the pocket chart. The teacher should make sure that students can read the strips to ascertain adequate sight word recognition and to determine the need for further instruction.

5. To develop competency in visual interpretation, students may wish to add an illustration to each sentence strip event of the story.

FURTHER READING

Cooper, J. D. (2000). *Literacy: Helping children construct meaning* (4th ed.). Boston: Houghton Mifflin.

Gunning, T. (2005). *Creating literacy instruction for all students* (5th ed.). Boston: Allyn & Bacon.

Reutzel, D. R., & Cooter, R. (2000). *Teaching children to read: Putting the pieces together* (3rd ed.). Columbus, OH: Merrill.

30 KWL

Also beneficial when working with English learners

Strategy at a Glance: *Grade Levels All*

When to Use	Grouping	Literature Type	Skill Areas
● before reading	○ individual	○ narrative	○ word recognition
● during reading	● small group	● expository	● vocabulary
● after reading	● whole class		● comprehension
	● center		● writing

Purpose

To engage students in creating meaning from text as they develop background knowledge, take ownership for learning, and organize information for retrieval

Literature Used

The Art of Ancient Egypt Under the Pharaohs, by Shirley Glubok

When to Use

Before, during, and after reading

Description of Strategy

In the acronym **KWL**, **K** stands for the "knowledge" already possessed by learners about a topic *before* reading begins; **W** represents "what" they want to learn *during* reading; and **L** stands for the information "learned" *after* reading or what may still need to be learned. Through the KWL strategy, students build and activate prior knowledge through brainstorming, asking questions about areas to investigate further, summarizing what they have learned, and determining what they need to extend their learning. This process occurs through teacher guidance in the form of a KWL chart.

Procedures for Use

1. The teacher introduces a new topic of study as well as the process of the KWL strategy. In this case, the topic is the art of ancient Egypt for a class of middle school

K—What I Know	W—What I Want to Know	L—What I Learned and Still Need to Learn

Categories of Information I Expect to Use

A.   E.

B.   F.

C.   G.

D.

FIGURE 30–1   Example of a KWL Chart

students. *Before* reading, the teacher explains the parts of KWL and each section of the chart. (See the example of a KWL chart in Figure 30–1.) The KWL chart for ancient Egyptian art contains all sections of a typical KWL graphic organizer except for the adaptation of pyramids representing "What I know" for **K**, "What I want to know" for **W**, and "What I learned and still need to learn" for **L**. Students record questions for the **K** and **W** columns on the pyramids, for the pyramids below the **L** columns, students record information learned. Pyramids may be added to each column as needed. (See the example for *The Art of Ancient Egypt Under the Pharaohs* in Figure 30–2.)

2. The teacher asks students to identify what they already know about ancient Egyptian art. They may record these responses on individual sheets, or they may give answers that the teacher writes on a transparency or chart paper for the entire class to see. Responses are recorded on the pyramids under the pharaoh head labeled "What I *know*" and may be recorded in abbreviated form. The teacher's role in this stage is to facilitate students' recall of what they think they know, not to determine the rightness or wrongness of the information. Some examples of student prior knowledge are as follows:

    a. They had lots of statues made out of stone.

    b. They had a Sphinx.

    c. They had beautiful gems and jewels (jewelry).

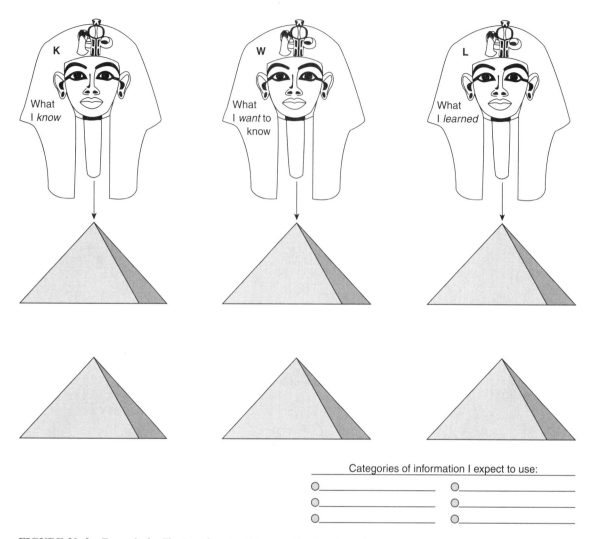

FIGURE 30–2 Example for *The Art of Ancient Egypt Under the Pharaohs*

    d. They used natural resources.

    e. They had great architects. Things were built for the weather and lasted a
       long time.

    f. The pictures they painted of people were very flat and had their heads turned
      sideways.

3. With teacher guidance, students generate questions concerning information they
   want to know about ancient Egyptian art. The teacher may need to model this stage
   of the process to get students started. Questions are recorded in the "What I *want* to
   know" column. Below are a few of these:

    a. Why did they wrap mummies?

    b. Why did they have a gold coffin to put mummies in?

    c. What's a pyramid? Are there houses or tombs in there? Is a tomb where you
      put a mummy?

    d. Why did they use so much makeup and make their faces look so weird?

    e. Do we really know enough about Egypt to ask questions?

4. The teacher should aid students in making connections between what they know
   already and questions they want answered by the reading. As this information is

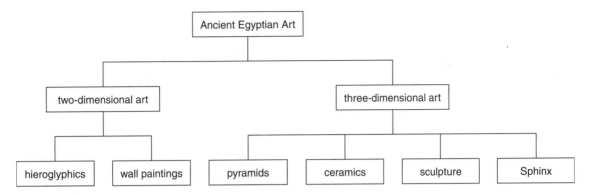

FIGURE 30–3   Example of a Thinking Tree for *The Art of Ancient Egypt Under the Pharaohs*

discussed, students should try to group ideas into categories. These should be listed on the KWL chart if students anticipate that the text will elaborate on them further. Based on prior knowledge and questions, some potential categories of information from *The Art of Ancient Egypt Under the Pharaohs* might be **statues, paintings, pyramids, jewelry**, and **burial customs**. The teacher and students may generate additional categories *during* reading in the next step.

5. The teacher directs students to read for answers to questions asked previously or to list information related to any of the categories generated. This phase is the **L** of the KWL process. Students may record what they have learned as they read, or they and the teacher may record their newfound knowledge once the reading is completed as part of class discussion. The teacher might use such prompts to foment discussion as:

   a. What have we learned from our reading?

   b. What came to mind that you still have questions about as you were reading?

   c. What were some new questions that came up as you read?

   d. Where can we write our new questions on the chart?

   e. Does any of the information from your reading fit into the categories we have on our chart—for example, *pyramids*?

   f. Do we want to add any new categories of information to our chart—for example, *burial symbols?*

6. Although not required, a final step might be for the teacher and students to create a graphic organizer to show main idea–detail relationships among information learned during the process of completing a **KWL**. For *The Art of Ancient Egypt Under the Pharaohs*, students categorized, in the form of a thinking tree, information learned under the headings of two-dimensional and three-dimensional art. This activity provided a way for them to summarize information visually so that they would remember it better. (See the example of the thinking tree for ancient Egyptian art in Figure 30–3.)

FURTHER READING

Cooper, J. D. (2000). *Literacy: Helping children construct meaning* (4th ed.). Boston: Houghton Mifflin.

Cooter, R. B., Jr., & Flynt, E. S. (1996). *Teaching reading in the content areas: Developing content literacy for all students.* Englewood Cliffs, NJ: Prentice Hall.

Cunningham, P. M., Moore, S. A., Cunningham, J. W., & Moore, D. W. (1995). *Reading and writing in elementary classrooms: Strategies and observations* (3rd ed.). White Plains, NY: Longman.

Gipe, J. P. (2006). *Multiple paths to literacy: Assessment and differentiated instruction for diverse learners, K–12* (6th ed.). Upper Saddle River, NJ: Merrill/Prentice Hall.

Graves, M., Juel, C., & Graves, B. (1998). *Teaching reading in the 21st century.* Needham Heights, MA: Allyn & Bacon.

Gunning, T. (2005). *Creating literacy instruction for all students* (5th ed.). Boston: Allyn & Bacon.

Johns, J., & Lenski, S. D. (2001). *Improving reading: Strategies and resources* (3rd ed.). Dubuque, IA: Kendall/Hunt.

Reutzel, D. R., & Cooter, R. (2000). *Teaching children to read: Putting the pieces together* (3rd ed.). Columbus, OH: Merrill.

Ruddell, R. B., & Ruddell, M. R. (1995). *Teaching children to read and write: Becoming an influential teacher.* Boston: Allyn & Bacon.

Vacca, R. T., & Vacca, J. A. L. (2005). *Content area reading: Literacy and learning across the curriculum* (8th ed.). Boston: Allyn & Bacon.

Wood, K. D., & Dickinson, T. S. (Eds.). (2000). *Promoting literacy in grades 4–9: A handbook for teachers and administrators.* Boston: Allyn & Bacon.

31 SQ3R

Strategy at a Glance: *Grade Levels 4–8*

When to Use	Grouping	Literature Type	Skill Areas
● before reading	● individual	○ narrative	○ word recognition
● during reading	○ small group	● expository	● vocabulary
● after reading	● whole class		● comprehension
	○ center		● writing

Purpose

To help organize, elaborate, rehearse, and remember important information from text

Literature Used

HBJ Science, by Elizabeth K. Cooper and others

When to Use

Before, during, and after reading

Description of Strategy

With this procedure, students learn how to study text and retain important information through *surveying, questioning, reading, reciting,* and *reviewing.* The acronym SQ3R stands for these five components.

Procedures for Use

1. Students will be studying the first chapter, "On a Spaceship to the Planets," from the third-grade textbook, *HBJ Science.* As part of the *before* reading survey of the chapter, they should read the introduction, summary, captions under illustrations and other visuals, key vocabulary words, and section headings within the chapter. In short, students should preview anything in the passage that will build background knowledge when they begin the reading phase of SQ3R.

2. *Before* reading, as students *survey* textual information, they should ask *questions.* For students unfamiliar with the process of SQ3R, the teacher should model how the two steps work together. For this passage, the teacher demonstrates how to turn section

headings into questions so that readers must actively look for answers. For instance, the heading "First Stop—Mercury" could become "Where is Mercury?" or "What is Mercury like?" The same questioning process may be demonstrated with key vocabulary in boldface or with captions under any graphics in the chapter. Students should record questions on a piece of paper.

3. *During* reading, the teacher instructs students to *read* silently to find answers to their questions. (This step is the first of the three Rs in SQ3R.) It is probably best, when students are first using SQ3R, to have them read one section at a time rather than the whole chapter. They can ask questions and find answers to longer text passages as they gradually become more independent with the process. Initially, however, there may be a great need for guided practice before independence is achieved.

4. *After* students complete their reading of a section, they try to answer (*recite*) their pre-reading question(s). The answer to "Where is Mercury?" might be "Mercury is the closest planet to the sun." The answer to "What is Mercury like?" might be "It is the hottest planet. It is so hot no plants or animals live there." Students should try to answer the questions without looking back at the text. If they can successfully answer questions once they have read the section, they are ready to write their responses.

5. If students are unable to answer a question, they should reread the section before going to the next one. This final step is the third **R** of the SQ3R—namely, the *review* portion of the process.

6. When students have completed one section of the chapter, they repeat the same procedure for SQ3R with the next section. The teacher may allow them to become more independent with each subsequent section.

7. Once SQ3R has been used for all of the first chapter, students should put away their texts and cover their notes. As a final grand review, they ask themselves the survey questions that they have already answered to determine if they can still recall vital information for each one. If they cannot, then further reading and reviewing of the text will need to occur.

8. The teacher should realize that the procedure may take a while for students to master and may require extensive practice and guidance. However, the process is well worth teaching to students in the elementary grades and beyond as a way to help them monitor and take ownership for their own learning.

FURTHER READING

Gunning, T. (2005). *Creating literacy instruction for all students* (5th ed.). Boston: Allyn & Bacon.

Harris, A. J., & Sipay, E. R. (1990). *How to increase reading ability: A guide to developmental and remedial methods* (9th ed.). New York: Longman.

Johns, J., & Lenski, S. D. (2001). *Improving reading: Strategies and resources* (3rd ed.). Dubuque, IA: Kendall/Hunt.

Reutzel, D. R., & Cooter, R. (2000). *Teaching children to read: Putting the pieces together* (3rd ed.). Columbus, OH: Merrill.

Robinson, F. (1946). *Effective study*. New York: HarperCollins.

Taylor, B., Harris, L. A., Pearson, P. D., & Garcia, G. (1995). *Reading difficulties: Instruction and assessment* (2nd ed.). New York: McGraw-Hill.

Tierney, R. J., & Readence, J. E. (2000). *Reading strategies and practices: A compendium* (5th ed.). Boston: Allyn & Bacon.

Tompkins, G. E. (2005). *Language arts: Patterns of practice* (6th ed.). Upper Saddle River, NJ: Merrill/Prentice Hall.

32 Mapping with Guided Reading Procedure (GRP)

 *Also beneficial when working with English learners*

Strategy at a Glance: *Grade Levels 4–8*

When to Use	Grouping	Literature Type	Skill Areas
● before reading	○ individual	● narrative	○ word recognition
● during reading	● small group	● expository	● vocabulary
● after reading	● whole class		● comprehension
	○ center		● writing

Purpose

To organize text so that students comprehend the interrelationships among ideas presented

Literature Used

"The Indians of the Southwest Develop an Advanced Society," from *Our Country: People in Time and Place,* by Herbert J. Bass

When to Use

Before, during, and/or after reading

Description of Strategy

Mapping is an organizational technique through which students visually represent connections among main ideas and supporting details from text. The main idea is placed in the center of the map from which supporting details branch. These in turn may become main ideas for other supporting details as the map connects general concepts to information that is ever more specific. Mapping improves comprehension at any stage of the reading process. If the teacher provides students a map *before* reading, it gives them an overview of information from a passage. *During* or *after* reading, they may add to the map new information that they have learned. As maps evolve *during* reading, they remind students how ideas develop and fit together from text. Completed maps *after* reading provide a summary and review to reinforce content.

Procedures for Use

1. The teacher introduces the topic of study, "The Indians of the Southwest Develop an Advanced Society," from *Our Country: People in Time and Place,* a text intended for

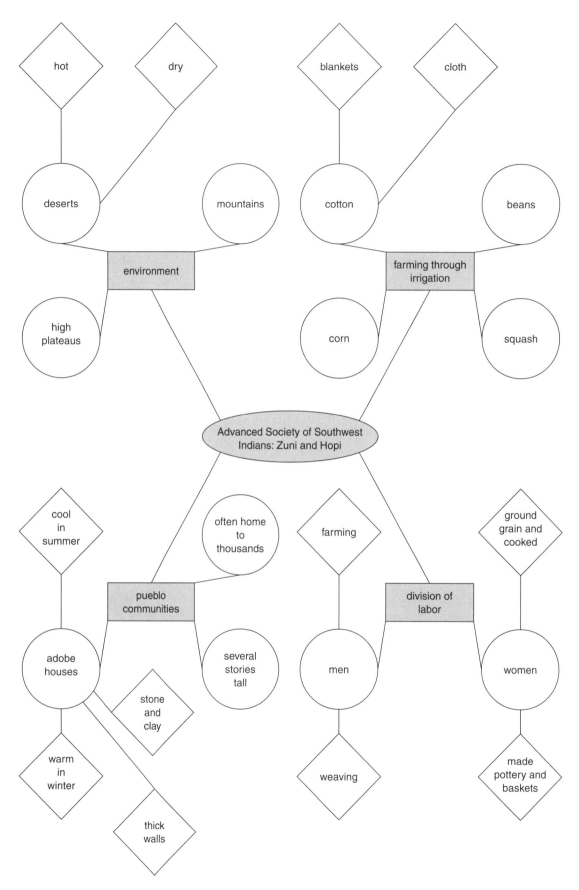

FIGURE 32–1 Example for "The Indians of the Southwest Develop an Advanced Society"

fifth grade. A version of this topic is written in the oval (or any preferred shape) in the center of the map, whether on the chalkboard, chart paper, overhead projector, or individual student sheets. As the main idea of the passage, it is the superordinate concept from which other ideas stem. (See the example for "The Indians of the Southwest Develop an Advanced Society" in Figure 32–1.)

2. At this point, the teacher may want to encourage students to ask questions that require them to hypothesize about the topic. One prompt might be "What do you think were some characteristics of Southwest Indian society?" Another might be "Who were the Indians of the Southwest and what were their lives like?" From these questions, students can make predictions about how these Indians built shelters, grew food, and worked. Students can also hypothesize about the natural environment of these people. Such predictions will stir curiosity and spur students to read the passage in an active search for information. For less capable learners, the teacher may read the passage aloud and ask them to listen attentively.

3. Students read (or listen) to gather details about how Southwest Indians lived. Students try to recall as many details as they can remember as the teacher or another recorder lists these for students to see. If any information is incorrect, the teacher directs students in purposeful rereading or has them listen again as portions are read aloud to clear up misconceptions. Together, the teacher and students modify the list until they are satisfied about its accuracy based on the text.

4. The teacher directs students to examine the list and to group ideas into categories by looking for common features. From the list, details fall into four major headings about Southwest Indians: environment, farming through irrigation, pueblo communities, and division of labor. These headings are major subordinate details for the overall topic and are coordinate with each other. To indicate this relationship, the teacher or students write these details in shapes that branch off from the main idea— in this case, boxes.(See Figure 32–1.)

5. The teacher and students now add details from the list that branch off from the appropriate supporting details. For instance, three details that go with the box "environment" are "deserts," "mountains," and "high plateaus." These are recorded in a different shape, here circles, again to show further subordination of details. The same procedure occurs for details that go with the boxed headings "farming through irrigation," "pueblo communities," and "division of labor."

6. If categorization is a major goal of the guided reading, *after* reading (or listening) students may tell all the facts they remember about Southwest Indians while the teacher records these on chart paper. These details are then cut apart, and students group them into categories and name the categories. From the categories and details, students create their own visual representation of a map with different shapes to indicate superordinate, coordinate, and subordinate ideas. (This process greatly resembles open sorts, described in the section on vocabulary, pages 60–63.)

7. After the map is complete, teachers may want to check for student understanding of the guided reading by giving a short quiz. Another follow-up activity might be to have learners take the information from the map and construct paragraphs with main ideas and supporting details, thus further developing competence in summarizing through writing.

FURTHER READING

Cooter, R. B., Jr., & Flynt, E. S. (1996). *Teaching reading in the content areas: Developing content literacy for all students.* Englewood Cliffs, NJ: Prentice Hall.

Vacca, R. T., & Vacca, J. A. L. (2005). *Content area reading: Literacy and learning across the curriculum* (8th ed.). Boston: Allyn & Bacon.

33 Reciprocal Questioning (ReQuest)

(EL) *Also beneficial when working with English learners*

Strategy at a Glance: *Grade Levels All*

When to Use	Grouping	Literature Type	Skill Areas
○ before reading	● individual	● narrative	● word recognition
● during reading	● small group	● expository	● vocabulary
● after reading	● whole class		● comprehension
	○ center		○ writing

Purpose

To promote comprehension through questions that the teacher and students take turns in asking one another

Literature Used

The Jolly Mon, by Jimmy Buffett and Savannah Jane Buffett

When to Use

During and after reading

Description of Strategy

ReQuest, or reciprocal questioning, develops comprehension because readers select information, ask questions about it, predict outcomes, and then confirm or reject their predictions. This reading-questioning procedure gives students the opportunity to improve their understanding of what they have read by letting them come up with questions to ask the teacher that resemble those they think the teacher might ask them. The strategy will work with one student or with larger groups. The teacher first models questions to students to guide them in getting meaning and to help them come up with thought-provoking questions that will allow critical thinking. Students are encouraged to reflect on what they have heard and read and to organize their reflections.

The strategy starts with the teacher stating the purpose. The teacher and students then read a sentence or group of sentences (no longer than a paragraph) silently. Students who do not comprehend well may need to read very short pieces of text. For nonreaders, the teacher may elect to read aloud only one or two sentences to which students listen before they ask the teacher questions. The teacher and students take turns asking questions. All questions asked deserve to be answered as fully and honestly as possible. If questions are unclear, requests for rephrasing are allowed. The responder can refer to the text to justify an answer but should have the book closed during listening and answering.

The teacher should actively attempt to model good questioning behavior. The teacher may have to stop, when questions are beyond the literal level, and may have to point out explicitly to learners what makes a question of a higher level than simple recall of information. This process continues until enough information has been gained for readers to make predictions about the remainder of the assignment. When the reading is completed, the teacher and students discuss whether the predictions were confirmed by the text. Purposeful rereading for clarification may be necessary.

Procedures for Use

1. The passage should have a reading level commensurate with that of the students. If not, the teacher may read orally to them. The passage should also contain enough information so that the students and the teacher can ask a number of questions about it.

2. *Before* reading, the teacher explains the ReQuest procedure and its purpose to students. "This lesson will help you understand better what we will read today. We will silently read our story, *The Jolly Mon*, by Jimmy Buffett and Savannah Jane Buffett. *After* we read parts of the story, we will take turns asking each other questions about it. You get to ask me questions first, and then I'll ask you some questions. When you ask questions, try to ask them the way I would ask them as your teacher. Try to make me think hard. You may ask as many questions as you like. We will keep our books closed as we ask each other questions."

3. At this point, the teacher may want to engage students in a brief survey of the book or do a short picture walk. (See pages 91–92.) Such a preview will motivate reader interest and will activate or build background knowledge. The teacher might read the title, analyze with students any illustrations that are part of the introduction, and get predictions on what the selection is about. The teacher might say "The cover of *The Jolly Mon* shows a young black man with long braids standing on a boat looking out to the green-blue sea. Also, the title uses the word 'Mon' instead of 'Man.' The author is a well-known singer/songwriter of Caribbean-style songs. All of these clues indicate that the story is about a young man from the Caribbean." If a map is available, the teacher may show the location of the setting.

4. The teacher instructs students to read the first significant segment of text silently and directs them to think of questions to ask. Students may make up as many questions as they want. The teacher silently reads the selection also.

5. All close their books. If needed, questions may be restated or clarified. Answers may be checked by looking back at the text. The story states, "Had it not been for the threat of the pirates, Bananaland would have been the most peaceful place on earth." A higher-order question a student might ask about this sentence is "Why do you think the island was called Bananaland?"

6. After students have asked questions, the teacher asks and models higher-level questioning. A question the teacher might ask is "What was dangerous about Bananaland and what does that imply might happen later in the story?" As the reading and questioning progresses, the teacher can explain difficult vocabulary or concepts.

7. The questioning continues after each passage is read until enough information has been assembled so that a purpose is set for reading the rest of the text without reciprocal questioning. A purpose question that requires prediction is: "What do you think will be the outcome of the story? Why?"

8. After the rest of the story has been read silently, the purpose question and any other questions about the story are discussed as students verify their predictions.

FURTHER READING

Cooter, R. B., Jr., & Flynt, E. S. (1996). *Teaching reading in the content areas: Developing content literacy for all students*. Englewood Cliffs, NJ: Prentice Hall.

Graves, M., Juel, C., & Graves, B. (1998). *Teaching reading in the 21st century*. Needham Heights, MA: Allyn & Bacon.

Gunning, T. (2005). *Creating literacy instruction for all students* (5th ed.). Boston: Allyn & Bacon.

Manzo, A. V. (1969). The ReQuest procedure. *Journal of Reading*, *11*, 123–126.

Reutzel, D. R., & Cooter, R. (2000). *Teaching children to read: Putting the pieces together* (3rd ed.). Columbus, OH: Merrill.

Ruddell, R. B., & Ruddell, M. R. (1995). *Teaching children to read and write: Becoming an influential teacher*. Boston: Allyn & Bacon.

Taylor, B., Harris, L. A., Pearson, P. D., & Garcia, G. (1995). *Reading difficulties: Instruction and assessment* (2nd ed.). New York: McGraw-Hill.

34 Comparison-Contrast Chart

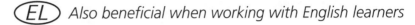

(EL) *Also beneficial when working with English learners*

Strategy at a Glance: *Grade Levels All*

When to Use	Grouping	Literature Type	Skill Areas
○ before reading	● individual	● narrative	○ word recognition
○ during reading	● small group	● expository	● vocabulary
● after reading	● whole class		● comprehension
	○ center		● writing

Purpose

To understand similarities and differences (or comparison-contrast) of events, ideas, or characters

Literature Used

A River Ran Wild, by Lynne Cherry

Pink and Say, by Patricia Polacco

When to Use

After reading

Description of Strategy

A comparison-contrast chart develops thinking skills as students discover how events, ideas, or characters are alike or different. The teacher creates a three-column chart. Elements of comparison or contrast for two general topics are listed in the center column. One general topic is written at the top of the left column and the other at the top of the right column. After reading, the students compare or contrast the specific elements of what they have read based on the elements given about the two general topics.

Procedures for Use

1. The teacher selects a book (or two books) that offers students an opportunity to compare and contrast.

2. *Before* reading, the teacher sets a purpose for reading by teaching the concept of comparison and contrast. This concept might be demonstrated with two students—height, outfit, hair color, and so on. This could be done, for example, with differences and similarities between fourth grade last year and fifth grade this year with such elements as homework, classroom, and lunchtime.

3. The teacher and students discuss the examples related to fourth and fifth grade. The teacher encourages active listening as students respond to questions related to comparison and contrast.

4. The teacher shows the students the prepared chart on an overhead or board. (See Figure 34–1.) After modeling the thinking for the first one or two examples, the teacher may let the students complete the chart in pairs or triads.

5. Once the background building discussion on comparison-contrast is complete, the teacher reads *A River Ran Wild*. The teacher instructs students to listen for differences in the thoughts of Native Americans and the thoughts of settlers, according to the book. (See Figure 34–2.)

6. *After* reading, the teacher distributes the prepared chart. The teacher may model the first item and let students complete the chart in cooperative learning groups. (See Figure 34–3 for another version of a comparison-contrast for Patricia Polacco's *Pink and Say*.)

Major Topic	Elements of Comparison-Contrast	Major Topic

FIGURE 34–1   Example of Generic Comparison-Contrast Chart

Indians (Native Americans)	Elements of Comparison-Contrast	Settlers (Non-Native Americans)
	use of animals	
	animal "feelings"	
	flow of the river	
	use of trees	
	land ownership	
	river ownership	
	care of natural resources	

FIGURE 34–2   Example of Comparison-Contrast Chart for *A River Ran Wild*

Pinkus	Elements of Comparison-Contrast	Sheldon
Pink	nickname	Say
	race	
	Union military weapons used	
	fought for the Union	
	education (reading)	
	prisoner of war	

FIGURE 34–3   Example of Comparison-Contrast Chart for *Pink and Say*

FURTHER READING

Gunning, T. (2005). *Creating literacy instruction for all students* (5th ed.). Boston: Allyn & Bacon.

Norton, D. E., & Norton, S. E. (2003). *Through the eyes of a child: An introduction to children's literature* (6th ed.). Upper Saddle River, NJ: Merrill/Prentice Hall.

Reutzel, D. R., & Cooter, R. (2000). *Teaching children to read: Putting the pieces together* (3rd ed.). Columbus, OH: Merrill.

Vacca, R. T., & Vacca, J. A. L. (2005). *Content area reading: Literacy and learning across the curriculum* (8th ed.). Boston: Allyn & Bacon.

35 Character Map

Strategy at a Glance: *Grade Levels 1–8*

When to Use	Grouping	Literature Type	Skill Areas
○ before reading	● individual	● narrative	○ word recognition
○ during reading	● small group	● expository	● vocabulary
● after reading	● whole class		● comprehension
	○ center		● writing

Purpose

To aid in recognizing and describing characters

Literature Used

Miss Nelson Has a Field Day, by Harry Allard and James Marshall

When to Use

After reading

Description of Strategy

Character maps are graphic organizers that help identify the different characters in a story and the words used by the writer that describe each character. Words may come from the text to describe the characters, or the words may be implied by the story or the pictures. A thesaurus will help students find synonyms for the descriptive words.

Procedures for Use

1. The teacher should select a book with at least three vibrant characters and no more than six to keep confusion minimal. *Miss Nelson Has a Field Day* has several interesting characters.

2. The teacher reads the story aloud, as students follow along, and directs them to listen for interesting things about the people in the story. At set points in the story, the teacher engages the students in guided listening by briefly pausing to comment on main characters or ask pertinent questions about them.

3. *After* reading the story, the students underline or write on another sheet of paper words or phrases that describe the characters. Students may refer to the book as part of purposeful rereading to learn details about each character.

4. Either the teacher or the students (with teacher guidance) draw a character map. (Refer to Figure 35–1.) The center of the map is a rectangle or any other preferred geometric figure that contains the story title. From the center, arrows radiate and connect to other shapes, usually ovals. Each oval has a character's name written in it. Triangles next radiate from each oval and will have words or phrases selected from the book or generated by the students themselves as descriptions of the various characters. These character descriptions may be stated or implied by the words in the text or suggested by its pictures.

5. A thesaurus will help students find synonyms for the descriptive words from the text and may become part of the character map. If the book says the principal was "goofy," a synonym from a thesaurus that might be added to the chart is "foolish." Use of a thesaurus fosters reader competencies in using reference tools.

6. An alternative approach is to have students draw the map on posterboard with different colored markers for character names and descriptors. The teacher might provide different colors of self-adhesive notes so that character names and

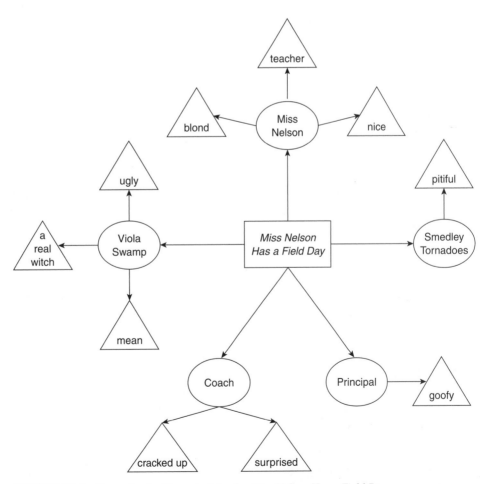

FIGURE 35–1   Example of a Character Map for *Miss Nelson Has a Field Day*

descriptors can be removed, mixed up, and placed back on the map. *Inspiration* software draws concept maps. Using this program as another alternative integrates technology into the lesson.

7. The teacher should provide for differences in pupil learning. Less able students may benefit from having a word bank of character names or descriptive words from the story. As an *after* reading extension activity, advanced students can write one or more sentences about a character like Miss Nelson by using the descriptive words found on the character map.

8. This strategy also works well with expository material when a class is studying famous people, places, or things in subject areas besides language arts.

FURTHER READING

Gipe, J. P. (2006). *Multiple paths to literacy: Assessment and differentiated instruction for diverse learners, K–12* (6th ed.). Upper Saddle River, NJ: Merrill/Prentice Hall.

Gunning, T. G. (2005). *Creating literacy instruction for all students* (5th ed.). Boston: Allyn & Bacon.

Johns, J., & Lenski, S. D. (2001). *Improving reading: Strategies and resources* (3rd ed.). Dubuque, IA: Kendall/Hunt.

36 Character Sketch

(EL) *Also beneficial when working with English learners*

Strategy at a Glance: *Grade Levels All*			
When to Use	**Grouping**	**Literature Type**	**Skill Areas**
○ before reading	● individual	● narrative	○ word recognition
○ during reading	● small group	● expository	○ vocabulary
● after reading	● whole class		● comprehension
	○ center		● writing

Purpose

To describe the thoughts, actions, experiences, and feelings of a character in a story

Literature Used

I Am Rosa Parks, by Rosa Parks

When to Use

After reading

Description of Strategy

A character sketch allows students to think about and write about a character's thoughts, feelings, actions, and experiences. The teacher duplicates a silhouette of a whole person or has students draw a silhouette of a person. *After* reading about someone, students will write about the person's thoughts in the head of the silhouette. The character's feelings will be written in the trunk (or body) of the silhouette near the heart. Things a character sees or hears may be added near the eyes and ears. Actions the character takes may be recorded on the hands. Places the character goes are added to the feet area. (See Figure 36–1.) Based on the information recorded on the character sketch, an extension of the strategy is for students to compose a summary paragraph for each attribute of the person. For instance, the paragraph could detail feelings taken from the trunk of the sketch.

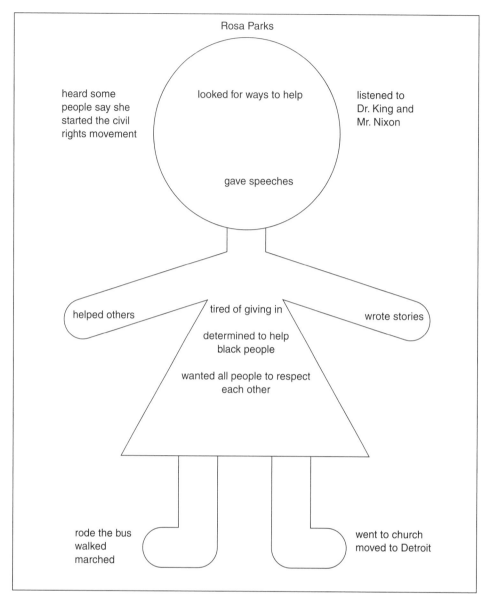

FIGURE 36–1   Example of a Character Sketch from *I Am Rosa Parks*

Procedures for Use

1. *Before* reading the story, the teacher should lead a discussion about how classmates have gotten to know each other. Remarks might include knowing classmates by what they do, what they say, or where they go. The teacher might use one student as an example. The teacher could explain that writers sometimes want readers to know about the people in a story, so readers have to pay attention to what writers say about the characters.

2. As a way to build background for the character sketch strategy, the teacher should show the book, *I Am Rosa Parks,* and may want to state, "This book is an autobiography. That means Rosa Parks wanted you to know her story, so she wrote this book." The teacher sets a purpose by telling students to listen *during* reading to learn as many details about Rosa Parks as they can remember.

3. *After* reading, the teacher shows Rosa Parks' silhouette on a poster and prompts the students to remember some places Ms. Parks went. Class responses are written by

the teacher on the feet of the silhouette. Prompts for the discussion about Rosa Parks might include questions like these: "What are some things she saw? What is something she heard? What did she do to help others?" As the students offer ideas from the text, the teacher models writing other responses on body parts of the silhouette.

4. Upon completing the silhouette with relevant details, students can use it to guide their writing of one or more paragraphs about the character. Like many graphic organizers, the character sketch functions as a prewriting outline for ordering one's thoughts.

5. This strategy works well collaboratively with a partner or small groups as well as independently for character study.

FURTHER READING

Carmine, D., Silbert, S., Kame'enui, E. J., Tarver, S. G., & Jungjohann, K. (2006). *Teaching struggling and at-risk readers: A direct instruction approach.* Columbus, OH: Merrill/Prentice Hall.

Gipe, J. P. (2006). *Multiple paths to literacy: Assessment and differentiated instruction for diverse learners, K–12* (6th ed.). Upper Saddle River, NJ: Merrill/Prentice Hall.

37 The Setting Book

Also beneficial when working with English learners

Strategy at a Glance: *Grade Levels 2–6*

When to Use	Grouping	Literature Type	Skill Areas
● before reading	○ individual	● narrative	○ word recognition
○ during reading	○ small group	○ expository	○ vocabulary
● after reading	● whole class		● comprehension
	○ center		● writing

Purpose

To help students determine the setting(s) of a particular piece of literature.

Literature Used

When I Was Young in the Mountains, by Cynthia Rylant

When to Use

Before and after reading

Description of Strategy

The setting book helps readers remember the setting(s) of a particular book they are reading. After the teacher activates prior knowledge about the where and when of setting, students will listen to the teacher read a book and answer questions about the setting. They will record their answers under each letter of the setting book. It has three pages. The first two pages have seven equal slits left to right. The slits are positioned so that they may be raised to reveal questions underneath. The first page, or the cover, has each letter of the word "setting" on each of the separate seven slits. The second page has questions related to student experiences and is used *before* reading. To illustrate the strategy with a specific story, the third page has questions from *When I Was Young in the Mountains* and is completed *after* reading.

Procedures for Use

1. The teacher prepares a setting book for each student. (See Figure 37–1.) Under each letter of the word "setting," questions will help activate student prior knowledge *before* reading. Questions include "Where do you go to sleep at night?" under the letter **s** "Where do you eat breakfast in the morning?" under the letter **e** "Where do you watch television?" under the letter **t** and so forth. Each student may have different answers. Students record their answers under each letter on the second page of the setting book where the prompts are. The teacher will explain to the students that the answers to each of their questions will be a setting. For example, the setting where the class is would be the classroom or perhaps the room number.

2. After each student has completed the second page of the book, the teacher will call on a few students to share their answers. Once sharing is done, the students will put their setting books aside, and the teacher will read *When I Was Young in the Mountains* by Cynthia Rylant. The teacher tells the students to listen for setting changes.

3. *After* reading the book to the class, the teacher asks students to get out their setting books. The third page of the book will contain questions about the setting of *When*

Sample Setting Book

S	e	t	t	i	n	g

Page 1 (Cover): There is a slit between each letter, so that the letters flip up to reveal the questions below:

Where do you go to sleep at night? Your response:	Where do you eat breakfast in the morning? Your response:	Where do you watch television? Your response:	Where do you play tag? Your response:	Where do you go after school? Your response:	Where do you eat dinner? Your response:	Where do you eat lunch at school? Your response:

Page 2: These questions are used *before* reading to activate prior knowledge. There is a slit between each question so that the sections flip up.

Where did Grandfather go to work? Your response:	Where did the girl and her grandmother walk at night? Your response:	Where did the brother and sister go swimming? Your response:	Where was the well where they pumped water? Your response:	Where did they go to church? Your response:	Where did the girl's grandmother shell beans? Your response:	What is the main setting of this story? Your response:

Page 3: This page is used *after* reading. There is no need for a slit between each section. Note that all three sheets need to be stapled together at the top and form "a book."

FIGURE 37–1   Example of a Setting Book for *When I Was Young in the Mountains*

I Was Young in the Mountains. The teacher will model how to answer the first question for the students. For guided practice, the teacher and students will complete the second question (under the "e") together. The class will do the rest of the book independently. Once students have finished, they may choose a partner and compare answers.

4. If less able learners are in the classroom, the teacher may work with these students or provide a concept bank from which they may select answers.

FURTHER READING

Frey, N., & Fisher, D. B. (2006). *Language arts workshop: Purposeful reading and writing instruction.* Columbus, OH: Pearson Prentice Hall.

Gipe, J. P. (2006). *Multiple paths to literacy: Assessment and differentiated instruction for diverse learners, K–12* (6th ed.). Upper Saddle River, NJ: Merrill/Prentice Hall.

Gunning, T. (2005). *Creating literacy instruction for all students* (5th ed.). Boston: Allyn & Bacon.

PART V

Writing Strategies

38 All About . . . Books

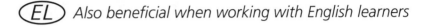

(EL) *Also beneficial when working with English learners*

Strategy at a Glance: *Grade Levels All*

When to Use	Grouping	Literature Type	Skill Areas
● before reading	● individual	● narrative	○ word recognition
● during reading	● small group	● expository	● vocabulary
● after reading	● whole class		● comprehension
	○ center		● writing

Purpose

To integrate reading, writing, and visual literacy through narrative text or through expository text

Literature Used

Prudence's Book of Food, by Alona Frankel

My Many Colored Days, by Dr. Seuss

When to Use

Before, during, and after reading

Description of Strategy

All About . . . Books may impart information as students write narratives about themselves or as they discuss informational topics in an expository mode of expression. In the first instance of narratives, All About . . . Books, done as autobiographies, are referred to as All About Me Books and give personal information such as date of birth; descriptions of family members, friends, pets, and other significant associates; favorite activities and books; interests; and so forth. In the second instance, if written as expository text about nonpersonal topics, All About . . . Books may be on such subjects studied in content areas as presidents, weather phenomena, insects, the circulatory system, a particular city like San Francisco, and so forth. In either case, illustrations accompany both types of All About . . . Books and allow students to express ideas through visual communication as well as through writing. These books also may aid students in developing strategic study competencies as they organize their final products into appropriate sections that include a title page, table of contents, numbered pages with synchronized words and pictures, and perhaps a bibliography of informational sources used in creating their work.

Procedures for Use

1. The teacher should select literature that will serve as a model for composing an All About . . . Book. For preschool and early primary age children, Alona Frankel's *Prudence's Book of Food* is appropriate for the content area of health and would serve as an example for learners to explore appropriate and inappropriate foods to eat. For older primary and intermediate-grade students, Dr. Seuss's *My Many Colored Days* would be a good choice for an autobiographical All About Me Book that discusses different personal feelings they have from time to time as these relate to moods of color.

2. *Before* reading, the teacher shares either story (or another one) with the students. As students listen, the teacher reads *aloud* and pauses to discuss how the pictures complement and supplement the meaning of the words. Students should feel free to join the discussion and add their own interpretations of pictures and words. For instance, with *My Many Colored Days,* students might describe how they react to what Dr. Seuss calls "Bright Red Days" or "Happy Pink" days.

3. The teacher may want to revisit the selected text a second time *during* reading by having the listeners join in as they read *along.* For extra practice, a third reading could occur as students read *alone* without the teacher's assistance. This shared mode of reading provides multiple exposures to the book's words.

4. Proceeding from literary models, the teacher and students now create either an All About . . . Book or an All About Me Book. If *Prudence's Book of Food* has been the model, preschool and early primary grade children may describe other types of appropriate edible foods for the content area of health. Their books might be titled *All About Foods.* If *My Many Colored Days* is the choice, primary or intermediate-grade students could title their works *All About My Many Colored Feelings.* Both works would have at least a single sentence or caption per page, and each page would have an accompanying illustration.

5. For whichever type of book students compose, the teacher may want to scaffold the writing through the language experience approach (LEA) as part of *after* reading. Working with individuals, small groups, or a whole class, the teacher engages learners in a conversation about the book's content (i.e., what kinds of foods to include and discuss or what types of personal feelings to match with different colors. (See pages 19–21 to find out more about the language experience approach.) Once learners reach consensus about content, they dictate to the teacher their captions for each page. The teacher records these on the chalkboard, chart paper, or overhead projector and reads the words *aloud* as students see their ideas unfold and thus develop competence in word recognition. Next, the teacher and students read *along* together the recorded text. Finally, students will read the captions *alone.* More advanced students may be able to write the captions themselves and create their books independently.

6. The teacher may direct students to a computer to use a word processing program to reproduce the captions in typed print. The teacher will begin by showing the student the different fonts on the computer. This procedure will help students to realize that words can look different if typed in different types of print. Then, students will read each caption while the teacher types it. Finally, the teacher and students will print out the captions. Students will cut out each caption and glue it to match the

appropriate picture they have created for their books. Instead of drawings, some students may want to illustrate their captions with photographs.

7. The teacher should make sure that the books, whether by individuals, small groups, or the whole class, are bound in some form. Pages might be connected with a plastic spiral ring binding. Books may be bound individually, or all may be bound as a class project for sharing with others whether students, parents, teachers, or administrators.

FURTHER READING

Tompkins, G. E. (2005). *Language arts: Patterns of practice* (6th ed.). Upper Saddle River, NJ: Merrill/Prentice Hall.

39 Story Impressions

Also beneficial when working with English learners

Strategy at a Glance: *Grade Levels All*

When to Use	Grouping	Literature Type	Skill Areas
● before reading	● individual	● narrative	○ word recognition
○ during reading	● small group	○ expository	● vocabulary
● after reading	○ whole class		● comprehension
	○ center		● writing

Purpose

To use clues to predict and then write story events that students later compare to the original story

Literature Used

Piggie Pie, by Margerie Palanti

When to Use

Before and after reading

Description of Strategy

Story impressions stir the curiosity of learners and activate their prior knowledge as they use teacher-provided clues to predict and construct their versions of a story *before* reading the original. Story impressions include key words or phrases of one, two, or three words related to the original story. These key words should represent character, setting, and major elements from the plot. The teacher should restrict the number of key words or phrases to approximately 10 to 15 for a short story or picture book and to around 15 to 20 for a chapter book. The clues should be arranged vertically with arrows or lines to indicate the sequence. The teacher should stress that students use the words in the order that they appear. Otherwise, students may get the events out of sequence. Story impressions become guideposts from which students make predictions or ask questions *before* reading.

Students use their background knowledge to hypothesize the story events. Working in small groups of three or four, they create their own story by recording the events. They then compare their rendition to the original story *after* reading it. Through arousing curiosity and building background, the strategy of story impressions enhances literacy competencies of prediction, understanding sequence, writing, and comparison-contrast.

Procedures for Use

1. The teacher shows the book *Piggie Pie* to the students.
2. Next, the teacher provides a general introduction such as, "Today we will make up what we think this story is about."
3. The teacher focuses student attention on the list of key concepts by saying, "Here are some clues about the story, *Piggie Pie,* that we will read." (See Figure 39–1.) "We

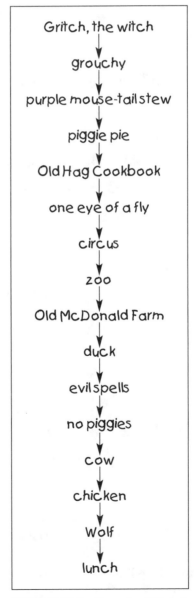

Gritch, the witch
↓
grouchy
↓
purple mouse-tail stew
↓
piggie pie
↓
Old Hag Cookbook
↓
one eye of a fly
↓
circus
↓
zoo
↓
Old McDonald Farm
↓
duck
↓
evil spells
↓
no piggies
↓
cow
↓
chicken
↓
Wolf
↓
lunch

FIGURE 39–1   Example of Clues for *Piggie Pie*

will use these clues to write our own version of the story. After that, we will read the story together to see if the author had similar ideas to ours."

4. After the students read the list of clues, they brainstorm, in small collaborative groups, about how the ideas might connect. The teacher lists the possibilities on the overhead or board.

5. The teacher allows the students to work in groups to come up with their own stories. (The students may work on a story individually.)

6. Using the brainstormed ideas, students develop a story that ties together the clues. (See Figure 39–2.)

7. The students read the author's actual story and discuss how their story compares and contrasts. A match with the author is **not** important. Instead, it is important to understand how the clues are woven together similarly or differently.

8. As an extension or follow-up activity for independent practice, students could work either in small groups or as individuals to develop stories based on clues from another text.

> Gritch the witch was grouchy. She put purple mouse tails in her stew. She put a pig in her pie. She made a gross witches cookbook. She was grouchy because she had to take the pie and stew to a lot of places. She took an eye out of a fly for the recipe. Then she took it to the circus, then the Zoo and Old McDonald Farm. She fed it to a duck. She put evil spells in it. She did not feed it to pigs. She put a cow in the rest of the stew. She fed it to a chicken. She put the wolf in the piggie pie. While she was eating lunch, she put an extra spell just for her and it made her un-grouchy.
>
> By: Shelbi   Grade 3

FIGURE 39–2   Example of Student Version for *Piggie Pie*

FURTHER READING

Gipe, J. P. (2006). *Multiple paths to literacy: Assessment and differentiated instruction for diverse learners, K–12* (6th ed.). Upper Saddle River, NJ: Merrill/ Prentice Hall.

Johns, J., & Lenski, S. D. (2001). *Improving reading: Strategies and resources* (3rd ed.). Dubuque, IA: Kendall/Hunt.

Tierney, R. J., & Readence, J. E. (2000). *Reading strategies and practices: A compendium* (5th ed.). Boston: Allyn & Bacon.

Vacca, J. A. L., Vacca, R. T., & Gove, M. K. (2000). *Reading and learning to read* (4th ed.). New York: Addison Wesley Longman.

Vacca, R. T., & Vacca, J. A. L. (2005). *Content area reading: Literacy and learning across the curriculum* (8th ed.). Boston: Allyn & Bacon.

40 Rewriting a Story from Another Point of View

 Also beneficial when working with English learners

Strategy at a Glance: *Grade Levels 4–8*

When to Use	Grouping	Literature Type	Skill Areas
○ before reading	● individual	● narrative	○ word recognition
○ during reading	● small group	● expository	○ vocabulary
● after reading	○ whole class		● comprehension
	○ center		● writing

Purpose

To promote understanding of the literary elements of genre, point of view, style, and character through writing

Literature Used

"The Frogs Who Wanted a King," by Aesop

When to Use

After reading

Description of Strategy

Genre, point of view, style, and character are important literary components for students to comprehend as they develop literary appreciation. All of these may be enhanced through writing activities in which students create their own versions of another story. As learners study genres such as fables, legends, myths, folktales, historical fiction, biography, modern realism, and others, they learn characteristics peculiar to each type of literature. In studying fables, students learn that these stories are usually short narratives, often having animal but sometimes human characters, and that the stories teach a life truth in the form of a moral either stated or implied.

Students also learn in their literature program about point of view, the four common types being omniscient, limited omniscient, first person, and objective. In the omniscient point of view, the narrator is all-knowing, capable of recounting not only all of the characters' actions and conversations but also their thoughts and feelings. The narrator tells about the story characters and speaks in third person. In the limited omniscient viewpoint, the narrator also speaks in third person, but this time reveals the thoughts and feelings of only one character. For all other characters, the narrator is limited to reporting action and dialogue. First person point of view elevates one of the characters in the story to the status of narrator and uses first person pronouns like "I," "we," "our," and "us." The narrator is an eyewitness to the story's events or reports events from hearsay passed on by other characters. In the objective point of view, the narrator returns to third person but reports just the facts and omits any personal interpretation so that readers must draw their own conclusions as to the meaning of events. Sometimes called the dramatic point of view, this form of telling a story is limited to conversation and action as in watching a play from which listeners must infer what characters think and feel.

Style of writing—that is, diction, sentence structure, imagery, and atmosphere—are all governed by point of view. Thus, a story told in first person may have a highly different style from one told in omniscient or objective point of view. If students rewrite in first person a genre story like the Aesop fable "The Frogs Who Wanted a King," they have the opportunity to experiment with word choice, sentence structure, figures of speech, and atmosphere as they transform a story originally told in omniscient point of view.

Aesop's "The Frogs Who Wanted a King"

Some frogs who lived in a pond were bored with freedom, so they sent a petition to Zeus and asked to be given a king. Although the god thought the frogs better off as they were, to oblige them he hurled a log into their pond. Hearing the splash, the frogs were terrified, and scurried to the pond's far corners. But by and by, seeing that the log lay motionless, they approached, and growing bolder said to one another, "What, is this our powerful king?" Soon they were jumping out of the water and squatting on the log, croaking in contempt.

After a while, they tired of this sport. Again, some of them went to Zeus and asked him to get rid of such a lazy, do-nothing king and send them a more forceful one. Annoyed, Zeus caused a great stork to descend to the pond. Frogs were his favorite food.

Example of a First Person Retelling of "The Frogs Who Wanted a King"

Dear gods and goddesses,

Let me tell you what these crazy frogs on Earth had the nerve to ask me, Zeus, the greatest god of all. They wanted a king. A king!!! Can you believe that? What could those lowly creatures want with a king? They are too low on the chain of existence to have their own king. Don't they know that I am Zeus, the all-powerful? I can create and destroy at the wiggling of my nose. But I decided to oblige those slimy creatures with their request. So, I thought about it and thought about it. Who or what would be a suitable ruler for those primitive creatures? I had it! I decided to send them a huge log to rule over them. Great idea, huh? This ruler would be understanding and lenient. The frogs could do whatever they wanted. I just knew that they would praise me for the selection I made. You know what I got from these pond dwellers? Nothing but grief. That's right! They said they wanted a forceful king. So, I decided to send a stork, one of the many enemies of all pond suckers. The stork loved his new kingdom, but the frogs didn't like their new king. That's what you get when you bother me when I could be doing better things. That'll learn 'em!

Yours truly,

The All-Powerful Zeus

The All-Powerful Zeus

FIGURE 40–1   Original Version and First Person Retelling of "The Frogs Who Wanted a King"

Procedures for Use

1. The teacher makes certain that students are thoroughly familiar with the original story—in this case, "The Frogs Who Wanted a King."

2. Other familiar children's stories and interpretations may also be discussed and shared with learners. These provide authentic models of how to write a different version of the same story.

3. An example to use for modeling rewriting may be "The Story of the Three Little Pigs" and some of the recent retellings. These examples are shared with students. The teacher may read aloud or have children read variations like Eugene Trivizas' *The Three Little Wolves and the Big Bad Pig,* illustrated by Helen Oxenbury; or Jon Scieszka's *The True Story of the Three Little Pigs! By A. Wolf,* illustrated by Lane Smith. The first version provides a model for rewriting the original story, while the second version demonstrates how one of the characters (the wolf) from the original tells his side of the story.

4. Once sufficient modeling and background building have occurred, students will be ready to rewrite the story under consideration. Figure 40–1 shows the original version of "The Frogs Who Wanted a King." It is followed by an example of an eighth grader's rendition in first person, with Zeus telling his side of things. The student's rewritten version in first person narrative uses a haughty style appropriate to the all-powerful Zeus and thereby conveys the disdain of the god for the bothersome frogs.

FURTHER READING

Donelson, K. L., & Nilsen, A. P. (1997). *Literature for today's young adults* (5th ed.). New York: Addison Wesley Longman.

Norton, D. E., & Norton, S. E. (2003). *Through the eyes of a child: An introduction to children's literature* (6th ed.). Upper Saddle River, NJ: Merrill/Prentice Hall.

Tompkins, G. E. (2005). *Language arts: Patterns of Practice* (6th ed.). Upper Saddle River, NJ: Merrill/Prentice Hall.

41 List and Five Senses Poems

EL Also beneficial when working with English learners

Strategy at a Glance: *Grade Levels All*			
When to Use	**Grouping**	**Literature Type**	**Skill Areas**
○ before reading	● individual	● narrative	○ word recognition
○ during reading	● small group	● expository	● vocabulary
● after reading	○ whole class		● comprehension
	○ center		● writing

Purpose

To develop literary appreciation for poetry, to teach main idea and detail organization in writing, and to enhance comprehension of narrative or expository text

Literature Used

"Swift things are beautiful . . . ," by Elizabeth Coatsworth, in *The Scott, Foresman Anthology of Children's Literature,* eds. Zena Sutherland and Myra Cohn Livingston

"Thanksgiving," by Ivy O. Eastwick, in *Ring Out Wild Bells: Poems about Holidays and Seasons,* ed. Lee Bennett Hopkins

When to Use

After reading

Description of Strategy

List poems help students to understand main idea-detail relationships and are one of the easiest kinds of poems to compose if learners are reluctant writers of poetry. Scaffolding of the writing process occurs through the formula that list poems follow. The key component of the formula is a verse paragraph structured according to a main idea and supporting details. The opening line(s) should convey a main idea statement usually in the form of a central image for each stanza of the poem. Students then list images that support the main idea of the key image.

Five senses poems follow the same structural concept as list poems, except that more scaffolding is provided through organizing each line around one of the five senses. These guide students in composing their list of images or figures of speech (namely, the details) for their verse paragraph.

Procedures for Use

1. For a list poem minus the five senses, Elizabeth Coatsworth's two stanzas of "Swift things are beautiful . . . " provide learners with a strong literary model. The opening line of the first verse illustrates its main idea: "Swift things are beautiful. . . ." The teacher makes this point with students.

2. The teacher then demonstrates how the remaining lines of the stanza contain a list of supporting details: swallows, deer, lightning, rivers, meteors, wind, horses, and runners. Although the poem rhymes, this feature is not necessary for students to include.

3. The next stanza of the poem begins with a contrasting main idea: "And slow things are beautiful. . . ." Again, a list of images follows containing details to support this main idea. Among these are the end of the day, the slow dying embers of a fire, the blooming of flowers, and a slow-moving ox.

4. After students have studied the structure of the main idea and supporting details, they may write their own list poems about topics studied in narrative or expository text. For example, they might compose a list poem about a main character in a story, a historical figure, a geographical place, or a concept in science or math.

5. For students who need additional scaffolding in writing a list poem, the teacher can show them how to incorporate images related to each of the five senses. Ivy O. Eastwick's "Thanksgiving" provides a good model if this way of structuring a list poem is used.

6. The teacher calls students' attention to the main idea of "Thanksgiving": namely, that each of the three stanzas has the key concept of being thankful for many of life's gifts. Although not all of the five senses are present, the first verse paragraph has the central idea of what the speaker in the poem is thankful for that "my hands can hold"; the second stanza for what "my eyes can see"; and the third for what "my ears can hear." Appropriate images follow as details to convey thankfulness for touch, sight, and sound in each stanza, respectively.

7. Once the teacher demonstrates the list structure related to the senses, students can create their own list poems around one or all of the five senses. The example from a second grader shown in Figure 41–1 is a five senses list poem about the main idea that "War is black." The teacher provided scaffolding by giving the students a simile for each sense listed for their chosen main ideas. These are "looks like," "tastes like," "feels like," "sounds like," and "smells like."

War

War is black.
War looks like bullets going through your heart.
War tastes like sand in your mouth.
War feels like a punch in the face.
War sounds like cannonballs whistling.
War smells like gas bombs.

FIGURE 41–1   Example of a Five Senses List Poem

FURTHER READING

Cunningham, P., & Allington, R. (1994). *Classrooms that work.* New York: HarperCollins.

Norton, D. E., & Norton, S. E. (2003). *Through the eyes of a child: An introduction to children's literature* (6th ed.). Upper Saddle River, NJ: Merrill/Prentice Hall.

Tompkins, G. E. (2005). *Language arts: Patterns of practice* (6th ed.). Upper Saddle River, NJ: Merrill/Prentice Hall.

42 Scamper

Strategy at a Glance: *Grade Levels All*

When to Use	Grouping	Literature Type	Skill Areas
○ before reading	● individual	● narrative	○ word recognition
○ during reading	● small group	● expository	● vocabulary
● after reading	○ whole class		● comprehension
	○ center		● writing

Purpose

To provide students with prompts to enhance creative rewriting opportunities about literature they have read

Literature Used

Cinderella (traditional)

The Egyptian Cinderella, by Shirley Climo

Cinder Edna, by Ellen Jackson

The Rough-Face Girl, by Rafe Martin

When to Use

After reading

Description of Strategy

SCAMPER is an acronym to help writers think of possible stories that could happen if the original version were modified in some way. Each letter in SCAMPER represents a word that helps learners with ideas for creative rewriting. The letters in SCAMPER represent the following: **S** for substitute, **C** for combine, **A** for adapt, **M** for modify, **P** for put to use, **E** for eliminate, and **R** for rearrange or reverse.

✁ **Procedures for Use**

1. The teacher discusses with students the traditional story of Cinderella and encourages them to point out how other versions read are similar to and different from the traditional story.

2. Explaining that writers often create a new story based on another story, the teacher describes how the word SCAMPER can help students to do the same thing.

3. The teacher goes through each letter of SCAMPER, explaining what each letter stands for and giving an example for each letter.

4. If SCAMPER is used with Cinderella stories, the following prompts are possibilities. Usually, the student selects only one or two of these to aid with rewriting:

   S substitute

      (What if Cinderella lost her handkerchief instead of her shoe?)

   C combine

      (What do Cinderella and Cinder Edna have in common? Can the two stories be combined in some way?)

   A adapt

      (What if the music at the ball had been so loud that Cinderella couldn't hear the clock strike midnight?)

   M modify

      (What would happen if the prince never found anyone whose foot fit the slipper?)

   P put to use

      (What will Cinderella do now with her remaining glass slipper?)

   E eliminate

      (What if there were no pumpkins for the godmother to use?)

   R rearrange or reverse

      (What if the godmother showed up after the ball? Begin your story with the marriage of Cinderella and the prince.)

Note: No reference has been found for this strategy; however, the authors have discovered it to be effective.

43 Imagery

EL Also beneficial when working with English learners

Strategy at a Glance: *Grade Levels All*

When to Use	Grouping	Literature Type	Skill Areas
● before reading	● individual	● narrative	○ word recognition
● during reading	● small group	● expository	● vocabulary
● after reading	● whole class		● comprehension
	○ center		● writing

Purpose

To enhance comprehension through writing or visual representation by guiding students in the development of mental images of text content

Literature Used

Owl Moon, by Jane Yolan

When to Use

Before, during, and after reading

Description of Strategy

Sometimes called "imaging" or "visualizing," imagery improves comprehension of text by encouraging students to create mental pictures *before, during,* and *after* reading and can also be a good activity to use *before, during,* and *after* listening to something read aloud by the teacher or other students. Imagery works especially well with descriptive passages in which the writer appeals to the reader's senses of seeing, hearing, feeling, tasting, or smelling. Activating prior knowledge, improving the ability to make predictions and draw inferences, and promoting overall listening and reading comprehension are among the benefits of using imagery. As with any strategy, the teacher should explain to students the purpose of visualization and why it will be beneficial.

⑧ Procedures for Use

1. The teacher selects a text rich in descriptive detail and, depending on the maturity and ability of students, reads aloud a sentence, paragraph, or longer passage. The beginning of Jane Yolan's *Owl Moon* is ideal for this purpose. The story describes a cold winter night when a little girl and her pa go owling and the moon makes the night sky shine brightly.

2. The teacher models the visualization process by creating visual images with students. This process occurs through think-aloud discussions. Mental images are then transferred to paper through drawing pictures (visual representation) or through writing. Sometimes, both pictures and writing may be used.

3. After modeling the process, the teacher initiates guided practice by reading another passage from the text and engaging students in a discussion of images that both they and the teacher visualize. Sufficient time should be allowed so that students can form appropriate and accurate images.

4. It is important not to alter the images created by students. However, the teacher may suggest that they reread or listen to the passage again and decide whether it should

FIGURE 43–1   Example of a Student Visual Representation for the Beginning of *Owl Moon*

be expanded and elaborated. These changes can be suggested through the judicious use of cues, prompts, and questions as part of scaffolding.

5. Independent practice should follow once the teacher feels confident that students have received enough scaffolding through guided practice. Again, students should have sufficient time to form images or to revise them through expansion or elaboration. The images may be shared through oral presentation, drawing, or writing, or through all three modes of communication. Figure 43–1 shows a drawing created by a student for the passage at the beginning of *Owl Moon.*

FURTHER READING

Taylor, B., Harris, L. A., Pearson, P. D., & Garcia, G. (1995). *Reading difficulties: Instruction and assessment* (2nd ed.). New York: McGraw-Hill.

Tompkins, G. E. (2005). *Language arts: Patterns of practice* (6th ed.). Upper Saddle River, NJ: Merrill/Prentice Hall.

Vacca, R. T., & Vacca, J. A. L. (2005). *Content area reading: Literacy and learning across the curriculum* (8th ed.). Boston: Allyn & Bacon.

44 Reluctant Writer

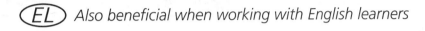

(EL) *Also beneficial when working with English learners*

Strategy at a Glance: *Grade levels 1–6*

When to Use	Grouping	Literature Type	Skill Areas
○ before reading	● individual	● narrative	○ word recognition
○ during reading	○ small group	● expository	○ vocabulary
● after reading	○ whole class		● comprehension
	○ center		● writing

Purpose

To provide scaffolding for children who are reluctant to be writers

Literature Used

Visiting Langston, by Willie Perdomo

When to Use

After reading

Description of Strategy

Some students are hesitant to write, or they lack ideas for writing. This strategy provides scaffolding with specific prompts to help generate ideas for writing.

Procedures for Use

1. The teacher selects either a narrative or expository book or a magazine or newspaper article. The strategy may work best with material that can be interpreted from a variety of viewpoints.

Examples from _Visiting Langston_

Langston Hughes was a writer. (fact)
Mr. Hughes wrote sad poems. (description)
I think he wanted people to be kind to each other. (feeling)

The little girl was a writer. (fact)
She wrote about things she enjoyed like hopscotch and jump rope.
   (description)
She was funny when she said she didn't like catch-n-kiss. (feeling)

FIGURE 44–1   Examples from _Visiting Langston_

2. The teacher introduces the book, _Visiting Langston,_ by showing the cover and title pages and by reading the information about Langston Hughes at the beginning of the book.

3. _Before_ reading the book aloud, the teacher sets a purpose for listening: "Listen carefully as I read this story aloud. Try to remember facts about Langston Hughes that you can describe and tell how they made you feel."

4. As the students listen, the teacher should stop periodically to encourage them to respond to the text and collage illustrations.

5. _After_ reading, the teacher asks the students to look at a transparency showing a written response to the text:

   a. The teacher recalls a _fact_ from the book and writes a sentence on a transparency, stating a fact about Langston Hughes. (The teacher may choose to write on a flipchart or the chalkboard.)

   b. The teacher uses a second sentence that _describes_ the _fact._

   c. The teacher writes a third sentence that records a personal _feeling_ about the _fact._

6. Once modeling is completed by the teacher, students may then work with a partner and create a three-sentence paragraph that _states another fact from the book, describes the fact, and gives a feeling about the fact._ Figure 44–1 shows modeling of a fact, description, and feeling written by the teacher. These are followed by a fact, description, and feeling written by a student team.

FURTHER READING

Cunningham, P., & Allington, R. (1994). _Classrooms that work._ New York: HarperCollins.

45 Innovative Text (Structured Rewriting or Patterned Writing)

(EL) *Also beneficial when working with English learners*

Strategy at a Glance: *Grade Levels All*

When to Use	Grouping	Literature Type	Skill Areas
○ before reading	● individual	● narrative	○ word recognition
○ during reading	● small group	● expository	○ vocabulary
● after reading	○ whole class		● comprehension
	○ center		● writing

Purpose

To provide students a partially completed framework or patterns for rewriting a familiar text to create individual innovations on it

Literature Used

"There Was an Old Lady" in *The Real Mother Goose Book of American Rhymes*, ed. Debby Slier

"Twinkle Twinkle Little Star" in *Jane Yolan's Mother Goose Songbook*, ed. Jane Yolan.

When to Use

After reading

Description of Strategy

The teacher selects a song or poem with which students are likely familiar. After the original text is read or sung, the teacher deletes key words. Students then work in small groups to create a new version by filling in alternative words in the blanks.

Procedures for Use

1. The teacher selects a familiar song ("Twinkle, Twinkle Little Star") and additional literature, such as "There Was an Old Lady," that can be adapted to fit this strategy.

2. Once the students are reminded of the song or poem, the teacher explains that the class will be rewriting it. For example, the teacher could show the words to "Twinkle, Twinkle Little Star" on a transparency, chart, or board. Students sing the song as the teacher points to the words. The teacher then displays the same song with key words deleted as illustrated below:

_____, _____ little _____,
How I wonder _____ _____ _____.
_____ _____ the world so _____
Like a _____ _____ _____ _____.
_____, _____ little _____,
How I wonder _____ _____ _____.

Oral responses from the students are recorded after they have discussed some possibilities for filling in the blanks.

Gliding, gliding little boat,
How I wonder how you float.
Moving in the world so wide
Like a fish who tries to hide.
Gliding, gliding little boat,
How I wonder how you float.

3. After this scaffolding has occurred, the teacher reads aloud the poem "There Was an Old Lady."

4. After listening, the class will have a copy of the words to the poem with key words deleted. Students work together to fill in the blanks. After writing, the groups may share the new version. (See Figure 45–1.)

5. Students can continue filling in blanks from other verses of this poem, since it continues for many stanzas, if the teacher wants them to.

There was an _____ _____ , she swallowed a _____ .
I don't know why she swallowed a _____ .
Perhaps she'll _____ .

There was an _____ _____ , she swallowed a _____ .
It _____ and_____ and _____ inside her.
She swallowed the _____ to catch the _____ .
I don't know why she swallowed a _____ .
Perhaps she'll _____ .

FIGURE 45–1   Example for "There Was an Old Lady"

FURTHER READING

Cooper, J. D. (2000). *Literacy: Helping children construct meaning* (4th ed.). Boston: Houghton Mifflin.

Cunningham, P. (2000). *Phonics they use* (3rd ed.). New York: Longman.

Cunningham, P., & Allington, R. (1994). *Classrooms that work.* New York: HarperCollins.

Reutzel, D. R., & Cooter, R. (2000). *Teaching children to read: Putting the pieces together* (3rd ed.). Columbus, OH: Merrill.

46 Concept Guides with Graphic Organizers for Main Idea-Detail Relationships

(EL) Also beneficial when working with English learners

Strategy at a Glance: *Grade Levels All*

When to Use	Grouping	Literature Type	Skill Areas
● before reading	● individual	○ narrative	○ word recognition
● during reading	● small group	● expository	○ vocabulary
● after reading	● whole class		● comprehension
	○ center		● writing

Purpose

To focus attention on the hierarchical arrangement of ideas (main ideas and supporting details) in written text

Literature Used

Scott Foresman Science, by Timothy Cooney and others

When to Use

Before, during, and after reading

Description of Strategy

Concept guides develop the notion that information is organized into superordinate concepts (main ideas) that have supportive subordinate details. These guides help students distinguish that some concepts are more important than others and that subordinate details may be categorized under dominate concepts that are main ideas. Concept guides consist of two parts. The first part asks students to recall important supportive details from a passage. The second part requires that these details be categorized under logical main idea headings.

This portion of the guide seems to work best for less able learners when it is constructed in the form of a graphic organizer like the ones in this book for a thinking tree, semantic map or web, or closed sort where the teacher has partially completed the graphic organizer to provide extra scaffolding. (See Figures 14–1, 15–1, and 18–1, respectively.)

Procedures for Use

1. The teacher analyzes a passage of text for hierarchical order where subordinate details are categorized within major concepts. The passage should contain key ideas that students need to learn and that they would more readily learn by determining the main idea-detail relationships within the text.

2. The teacher defines what is meant by the main idea and details. The main idea of a passage is the overall concept around which the passage is organized. The details of the passage should be related to the main idea and provide examples, elaboration, or support for it. The teacher next models through a think-aloud how to select the main idea and supporting details for a sample passage before students work through a concept guide so that they will have had schema built for using the strategy.

3. For the first part of the concept guide, the teacher selects key supportive details that logically may be grouped later into main idea headings. The important details are written in the form of statements to which students react by putting a ✓ beside the statement if contained in the reading. Students put an **X** beside statements not in the reading. (See Figure 46–1, Part A, for examples of key details derived from the sections, "How Do Insects and Spiders Grow?" and "How Do Fishes, Frogs, and Mammal's Grow?" from the third-grade text, *Scott Foresman Science.*)

4. Upon completing the first part of the concept guide on important details, the teacher develops the second part that requires categorization of information into superordinate, coordinate, and subordinate levels of support. Figure 46-1, Part B, contains the superordinate concept "life cycles." "Mammal," "amphibian," and "insect" are subordinate to it but are coordinate with one another. "Frog" is provided as an additional subordinate detail to its superordinate category "amphibian" so as to give further scaffolding.

5. To complete Part B, students select details from the concept bank (Figure 46-1) and place them under logical main idea categories. As added scaffolding, the word bank lets students know that some details may be used more than once as is indicated by the number in parentheses following "butterfly," "adult," and "egg."

6. While the concept guide in Figure 46-1 was used as an *after* reading review activity, a good idea in using concept guides with students is to have them preview the guide *before* they begin the assigned reading so they will read for a purpose. *During* reading, they complete the guide to help them navigate and organize main idea-detail relationships. *After* reading, students may verify the accuracy with which they completed the guide through discussion in small collaborative learning groups or through whole group verification under the guidance of the teacher. Such multiple exposures to the important information from the text will help implant it into long-term memory more efficiently than would merely assigning pages to read minus the scaffolding of the concept guide.

7. Once students have finished the graphic organizer part of the guide, the teacher may want to have them construct paragraphs with main ideas and supportive details. This writing extension based on what students have read will reinforce the learning of content information and teach the important study strategy of summarizing.

8. Some teachers and students may prefer to use a helping hand visual as an alternative to the graphic organizer in Part B of Figure 46-1. Figure 46–2 shows how a helping hand

Concept Guide for "How Do Spiders and Insects Grow" and "How Do Fishes, Frogs, and Mammals Grow?"

Part A

Directions: Look at each of the statements below. Based on what you read from pages A36–A47 of your science book, mark the statements which are correct by putting a ✓ mark beside the statement. If the statement is incorrect, put an X.

_____ 1.   Insects are the largest group of animals.
_____ 2.   Grasshoppers, crickets, and dragonflies have a four stage life cycle.
_____ 3.   Amphibians are animals that live part of their lives on land and part in the water.
_____ 4.   Fish need oxygen to live.
_____ 5.   Mammal mothers produce water to feed to their babies.
_____ 6.   Spiders belong to the animal group arachnids.
_____ 7.   Spiders and insects have bones.
_____ 8.   The pupa is part of a butterfly's life cycle.
_____ 9.   Gills are used by fish to get oxygen out of the water.
_____ 10.   A frog is a tadpole before it becomes an egg.
_____ 11.   Mammals have backbones and fur or hair.
_____ 12.   Whiskers are used by mammals to feel things around them.
_____ 13.   All mammals have only one baby at a time.

Part B

Directions: Use the concept bank below to complete the graphic organizer. You may want to refer to your textbook (pages A36–A47) for help. The words in the concept bank with ( ) show how many times that detail will be used in the graphic organizer. For instance, "butterfly" is followed by (2), so you would use it two times in the graphic organizer.

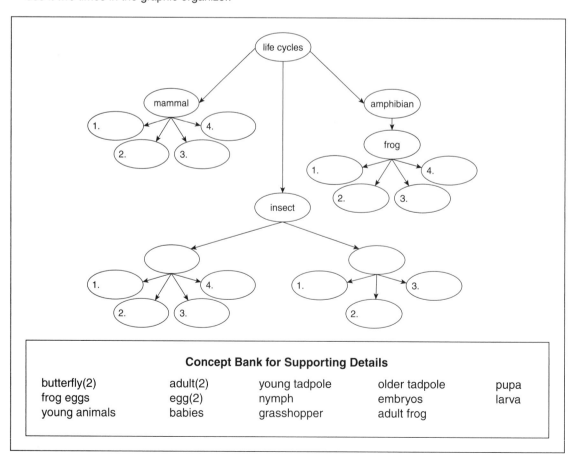

Concept Bank for Supporting Details

butterfly(2)	adult(2)	young tadpole	older tadpole	pupa
frog eggs	egg(2)	nymph	embryos	larva
young animals	babies	grasshopper	adult frog	

FIGURE 46–1   Example for *Scott Foresman Science*

Helping Hand for Summarizing Main Ideas and Supporting Details

Directions: Write a main idea or overall summary statement about the life cycle of insects that we have read about on pages A38–A39 from *Scott Foresman Science*. Write the main idea on the palm of the hand. Then write four supporting details about the butterfly's life cycle on the thumb and the fingers. Refer to your book to help you summarize the key information.

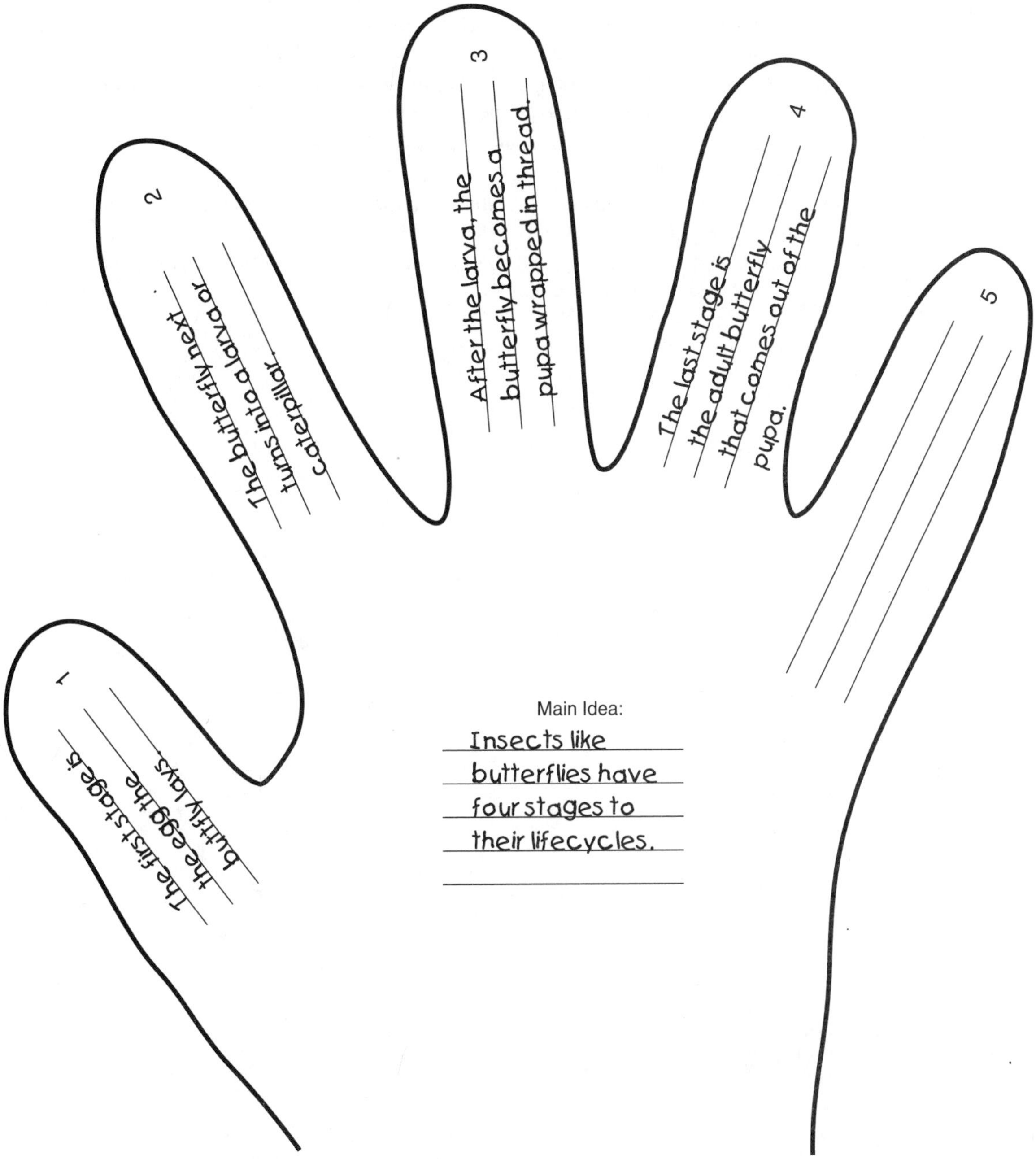

1

The first stage is the egg the butterfly lays.

2

The butterfly next turns into a larva or caterpillar.

3

After the larva, the butterfly becomes a pupa wrapped in thread.

4

The last stage is the adult butterfly that comes out of the pupa.

5

Main Idea:

Insects like
butterflies have
four stages to
their lifecycles.

FIGURE 46–2   Example for *Scott Foresman Science*

would work to aid learning to perceive main idea-detail organization. In this example, a superordinate concept is written in the palm of the helping hand, and subordinate ideas are recorded on the finger of the hand. As indicated in the previous procedural step, helping hands can serve as prewriting outlines to aid students in constructing summary paragraphs with a topic sentence containing a main idea followed by supportive details. In the case of the information from *Scott Foresman Science*, students would create several helping hands for such main ideas as "mammal," "amphibian," and "insect."

FURTHER READING

Baker, R. (1977). The effects of informational organizers on learning and retention, content knowledge, and term relationships in ninth grade social studies. In H. L. Herber & R.T Vacca (Eds.), *Research in reading in the content areas: Third report* (pp. 148–149). Syracuse, NY: Syracuse University Reading and Language Arts Center.

Brozo, W. G., & Simpson, M. L. (1999). *Teachers, readers, learners: Expanding literacy across the content areas* (3rd ed.). Columbus, OH: Prentice Hall.

Gipe, J. P. (2006). *Multiple paths to literacy: Assessment and differentiated instruction for diverse learners, K–12* (6th ed.). Upper Saddle River, NJ: Merrill/Prentice Hall.

Roe, B. D., & Smith S. H. (2005). *Teaching reading in today's middle schools*. Boston: Houghton Mifflin.

Roe, B. D., Stoodt, B. D., & Burns, P. C. (2001). *Secondary school literacy instruction: The content areas* (7th ed.). Boston: Houghton Mifflin.

Tierney, R. J., & Readence, J. E. (2000). *Reading strategies and practice: A compendium* (5th ed.). Boston: Allyn & Bacon.

47 Diamantes for Contrast Writing

Strategy at a Glance: *Grade Levels 2–8*

When to Use	Grouping	Literature Type	Skill Areas
○ before reading	● individual	● narrative	○ word recognition
○ during reading	● small group	● expository	● vocabulary
● after reading	● whole class		● comprehension
	○ center		● writing

Purpose

To provide students a framework or structure to follow as they contrast two story characters, real people, places, events, or concepts previously read or studied

Literature Used

Stone Fox, by John Reynolds Gardiner
A Man For All Seasons, by Robert Bolt

When to Use

After reading

Description of Strategy

A diamante (dee ah MAHN tee) is a poem shaped in the form of a diamond consisting of seven lines. This poetic form will aid students in comprehending differences and provide a structure for organizing two contrasting characters from stories, people from history, places, events, or concepts. Thus, diamantes work well whether students are writing about narrative or expository text that they have encountered. An added benefit of writing diamantes is that they reinforce knowledge of formal grammar if learners have been studying parts of speech or the functions of words in written work.

§ Procedures for Use

1. *Before* studying *Stone Fox*, the teacher instructs the students to pay close attention to the characters and to note opposite traits that they may have. For example, students might note differences between Little Willie and Grandfather. Students should brainstorm and record these ideas for later reference as they read through the story or hear it read aloud.

2. Either *before* or *after* the story is read, the teacher explains the purpose and structure of a diamante. "When we finish reading *Stone Fox*, you will write a diamante, or a poem in the shape of a diamond, that will contrast, or show the differences, between two characters in the book. Here's how your diamante will be organized."

3. The teacher then goes over the form of the diamante and how it will contrast two characters:

    a. The first line states the name of one of the two characters.

    b. The second line has two adjectives or words that describe this character in the first line.

    c. The third line uses three verbs, or action words, that end in *-ing* and that also describe the same character.

    d. The fourth line has two nouns that give other names to the character cited in line one. These two names are followed by two nouns that are additional ways to name the second character who is the opposite, or different, from the first character. A semicolon separates the contrasting descriptions of the two characters.

    e. The fifth line contains three words, again ending in *-ing,* that tell about the opposite second character.

    f. The sixth line uses two adjectives about the opposite character.

    g. The last line now gives the name of the second character.

4. To provide further scaffolding, the teacher may want to model for the class how to write a diamante that fulfills the required structure of the poem. This example could be based on two opposite characters from a previous story the students have read.

5. Once demonstration or modeling by the teacher has occurred, students write their own diamantes that contrast two opposite characters in *Stone Fox*. Figure 47–1 illustrates one student's diamante contrasting Little Willie and Grandfather. This example follows fairly faithfully the prescription for diamantes given in step 3.

6. Figure 47–2 provides a further example of a diamante that a collaborative learning group of older, eighth-grade students created *after* they had read and studied Robert Bolt's play *A Man for All Seasons*. This diamante contrasts the opposites Sir Thomas More and his enemy, Thomas Cromwell.

Little Willie
Brave, determined
Outgoing, farming, racing
Searchlight; Grandfather, race, sled
Winning, intimidating, caring
Cold, statue-like
Stone Fox

FIGURE 47–1   Example of a Diamante for *Stone Fox*

```
                    Sir Thomas More
                Compassionate, courageous
              Nurturing, forgiving, encouraging
              Nobleman, martyr; flatterer, bully
                   Climbing, lying, spying
                   Dangerous, insincere
                     Thomas Crowell
```

FIGURE 47–2   Example of a Diamante for *A Man for All Seasons*

FURTHER READING

Combs, M. (2006). *Readers and writers in primary grades: A balanced and integrated approach, K–4* (3rd ed.). Upper Saddle River, NJ: Merrill/Prentice Hall.

Sampson, M. B., Rasinski, T. V., & Sampson, M. (2003). *Total literacy: Reading, writing, and learning* (3rd ed.). Belmont, CA: Wadsworth/Thomson.

Tempke, C., Martinez, M., Yokota, J., & Naylor, A. (2002). *Children's books in children's hands: An introduction to their literature* (2nd ed.). Boston: Allyn & Bacon.

Tompkins, G. E. (2005). *Language arts: Patterns of practice* (6th ed.). Upper Saddle River, NJ: Merrill/Prentice Hall.

Tompkins, G. E. (2006). *Literacy for the 21st century: A balanced approach* (4th ed.). Upper Saddle River, NJ: Merrill/Prentice Hall.

48 Haiku for Summarizing Story Grammar Components

Purpose

To improve descriptive writing through brief text summaries of selected story grammar components

Literature Used

The Whales' Song, by Dyan Sheldon

When to Use

After reading

Description of Strategy

Haiku is a fixed form of Japanese poetry consisting of three lines. Each line has a set number of syllables. The first line has five syllables; the second line, seven; and the third line, five. These syllable restrictions narrow the word choices the writer may use to get the required count and may prove challenging. To help overcome this difficulty, the teacher will want to have several copies of a thesaurus available in the classroom. To aid further with the writing, the teacher can prescribe for each line of the haiku a story grammar element on which the students will focus: setting, characters, problem, key events, resolution, or theme. For instance, the first line might describe the main character of the story or book, while the second line summarizes a major event of the plot, as the last line states the theme. Reluctant writers may select for themselves the particular story grammar components that they will summarize in each line of the haiku. The writing may be done *after* reading by individual students needing additional reinforcement of story grammar, or it may be done by collaborative learning groups or by the entire class under teacher guidance. In the last instance, the haiku becomes like a language experience activity similar to the one described in Strategy 5 in the section on word recognition (pg. 19–21). Once discussion of final wording has occurred, the teacher can copy the finished class haiku and have the class read it.

Procedures for Use

1. The teacher selects a narrative like Dyan Sheldon's *The Whales' Song* to share with students and provides appropriate information to build background and stir interest in the text *before* reading.

2. *During* reading, the teacher asks questions to focus attention on story grammar. Typical questions might be "Who is this story about?" for main character; "Where does the story take place?" for setting; "What is Lilly and her grandmother's main conflict with Great Uncle Frederick?" for story problem; "What happens after Lilly hears Great Uncle Frederick's advice?" for resolution; or "What do you think we can learn from the conflict between the beliefs of Lilly's grandmother and great uncle?" for theme.

3. If students are not familiar with haiku, the teacher will also want to explain its characteristics, share some examples, and give the purpose for which students will be using it—namely, to summarize elements of story grammar. This explanation could occur during the *before* reading stage as schema building for the strategy that will later be used *after* reading.

4. For students unfamiliar with writing haiku to summarize story grammar, the teacher may want to give additional scaffolding by labeling each line with the specific story grammar component that learners are to summarize. The first line might be labeled "main character"; the second, as "major event"; and the third, as "theme." The following are two examples of haiku for *The Whales' Song*. Both show prescribed labels for each of the three lines of the poem:

Main character:	Lilly was a girl
A major event:	Who heard whales singing to her.
Theme:	Dreams are important.

A character:	Uncle Frederick
A major event:	Said singing whales were foolish.
Resolution:	Lilly kept her dreams.

5. In these two examples, fourth-grade students worked in small cooperative learning groups. Under the teacher's guidance, they revised their poems several times to be sure they focused on the story grammar component prescribed and to get the correct syllable count for each line. However, syllable count should not become a major impediment to the writing as long as students accurately describe the element of story structure and are fairly close to the required number.

6. After students have written haiku under teacher guidance and gotten used to the process, they may want to compose their own individual poems with self-selected

story grammar parts. As writers, they also may enjoy creating their poems on electronic authoring systems and illustrating their work. Writing haiku under teacher guidance to summarize story structure may eventually lead students to compose individual poems on any topic of their choosing and to publish class books.

FURTHER READING

Hopkins, L. B. (1987). *Pass the poetry, please!* New York: Harper & Row.

Strickland, D. S., Galda, L., & Cullinan, B. E. (2004). *Language arts: Teaching and learning.* Belmont, CA: Wadsworth/Thomson Learning.

Tompkins, G. (2005). *Language arts: Patterns of practice* (6th ed.). Upper Saddle River, NJ: Merrill/Prentice Hall.

49 Clerihews and Bio-Poems for Descriptive Writing

(EL) *Also beneficial when working with English learners*

Strategy at a Glance: *Grade Levels 2–8*

When to Use	Grouping	Literature Type	Skill Areas
○ before reading	● individual	● narrative	○ word recognition
○ during reading	● small group	● expository	● vocabulary
● after reading	● whole class		● comprehension
	○ center		● writing

Purpose

To give students a framework or structure to follow as they summarize details about people, events, or things previously read or studied

Literature Used

South Carolina: Its History and Geography, by Paul Horne, Jr.
Charlie and the Chocolate Factory, by Roald Dahl, Jr.

When to Use

After reading

Description of Strategy

Like list poems, five senses poems, and haiku (see Strategies 41 and 48, respectively), both Clerihews and bio-poems offer writers a framework around which to organize their details for a description or summary of someone or something from a topic previously studied or a text previously read. The reading may be narrative or expository.

Clerihews are poems of four lines and are named after the British detective writer Edmund Clerihew Bentley, the inventor of the form. Originally lighthearted poetry about the famous, Clerihews may be on any topic: storybook characters, people from history, places in geography, scientific concepts, animals, or personal descriptions of students themselves.

The form consists of four lines with the first two a rhyming couplet and the last two a rhyming couplet. The first line should state the name of the person, place, animal, or concept being described. The following procedures give the requirements for the remaining three lines.

Bio-poems provide students a more extended structure than Clerihews in the form of a prescription to follow for what each line should contain. The poem may be longer or shorter, depending upon the ability levels of the students or the teacher's purpose in prescribing the content of the lines. Bio-poems are unrhymed and are usually autobiographical descriptions of the students themselves, but like Clerihews they may be on any topic studied or read about in any school subject.

Procedures for Use

1. *After* reading and studying about various towns and communities in *South Carolina: Its History and Geography,* a third-grade teacher and her students decided to write Clerihews about their local city of Rock Hill, South Carolina. In preparation for the students to write, the teacher explained that the purpose of the Clerihews was to describe the home town where the students live. Students were directed to think about details and characteristics of Rock Hill from which they could select to include in their poems.

2. The teacher then explained the form of the Clerihew. The first line should be the name of the city, Rock Hill. The second line should rhyme with the first and have a detail about the city. The third and fourth lines should rhyme and contain additional details.

3. Figure 49–1 illustrates a Clerihew that one student wrote describing the traffic congestion in Rock Hill.

4. For teachers who want greater elaboration in student writing, the following pattern or prescription shows the usual details included in each line of a bio-poem of personal description:

    Line 1 – First name

    Line 2 – Three or four words that describe you

    Line 3 – Relative (brother, son, sister, daughter) of

    Line 4 – Admirer of (three things or people)

    Line 5 – Who feels (three items)

    Line 6 – Who needs (three items)

    Line 7 – Who fears (three items)

    Line 8 – Who gives (three items)

    Line 9 – Who would like to see (three items)

    Line 10 – Resident of (address)

    Line 11 – Last name

Rock Hill,
A place to chill.
With so much traffic to survive,
How do the people stay alive?

FIGURE 49–1　Example of a Clerihew

_____
(First name)

_____
(Three words that describe you)

_____
(Daughter/son of)

Who likes _____

Who feels sad when _____ and

Happy when _____

Who needs _____

Who gives _____

Who fears _____

Who would like to see _____

_____

_____
(City, State where you live)

_____
(Last name)

FIGURE 49–2　Example of a Bio-Poem as a Student Autobiography

Charlie
Beloved, hungry, honest, kind
Son of Mr. And Mrs. Bucket
Who loves chocolate and Grandpa Joe
Who feels lucky, excited, and grateful
Who needs food, a bed, a bigger house
Who fears losing the Grand Prize
Who wants to see the Wonka Chocolate Factory
Resident of a small house on the edge of town
Bucket

FIGURE 49–3　Example of Character Analysis Bio-Poem for *Charlie and the Chocolate Factory*

5. This prescription may be altered by adding other lines deemed important by the teacher (or students) or by subtracting lines. Figure 49–2 shows a teacher's modification of the pattern given in step 4 above.

6. Teachers may shift the autobiographical nature of the line requirements of bio-poems so that the writing focuses on a descriptive summary of a character, place, event, thing, or concept studied in a subject area. Figure 49–3 is an example of a bio-poem in which a fourth grader has written a thumbnail character sketch of Charlie Bucket in Roald Dahl's *Charlie and the Chocolate Factory*.

FURTHER READING

Combs, M. (2006). *Readers and writers in primary grades: A balanced and integrated approach, K–4* (3rd ed.). Upper Saddle River, NJ: Merrill/Prentice Hall.

Strickland, D. S., Galda, L., & Cullinan, B. E. (2004). *Language arts: Teaching and learning.* Belmont, CA: Wadsworth/Thomson Learning.

Tompkins, G. E. (2005). *Language arts: Patterns of practice* (6th ed.). Upper Saddle River, NJ: Merrill/Prentice Hall.

Vacca, R. T., & Vacca, J. A. L. (2005). *Content area reading: Literacy and learning across the curriculum* (8th ed.). Boston: Allyn & Bacon.

50 Letter Writing

EL Also beneficial when working with English learners

Strategy at a Glance: *Grade levels 4–8*

When to Use	Grouping	Literature Type	Skill Areas
○ before reading	● individual	● narrative	○ word recognition
● during reading	○ small group	● expository	○ vocabulary
● after reading	○ whole class		● comprehension
	○ center		● writing

Purpose

To use descriptive writing to improve understanding of such topics as people, places, animals, and other subjects that students encounter in narrative or expository text

Literature Used

Crispin: The Cross of Lead, by AVI

When to Use

During or after reading

Description of Strategy

During or *after* reading a narrative or expository passage, students write a letter describing a person, place, thing, or animal related to the reading. Students couch their descriptions in the form of a letter to a friend, teacher, community member, story character, person from history, or any interested party. Letter writing of this sort requires learners to focus on an audience and to provide accurate information in their descriptions.

Procedures for Use

1. In a study of the Middle Ages, a sixth-grade world history teacher used AVI's novel *Crispin: The Cross of Lead* as a parallel to the chapter in the social studies book.

2. As a writing-to-learn activity, the students were to send a letter to one of the characters in the novel and describe a facet of contemporary life that would contrast to an aspect of life at the time of the Black Death in medieval England.

3. One student chose to write to the main character, Crispin, and to describe the differences between a fast food restaurant and the Green Man tavern in the medieval city of Great Wexly. The following is this writer's finished letter:

> October 25, 2005
>
> Dear Crispin,
>
> Now that your adventures are over, I hope your life is easier than it was at the beginning of the story. You went through a lot as a serf at the manor house. You had many adventures as a "wolf's head" or outlaw when anybody could kill you, no questions asked.
>
> Anyway, I wanted to tell you about the kinds of places we have to eat where I live in this modern world. They are a lot different from the Green Man tavern where you stayed with Bear in Great Wexly.
>
> At my favorite fast food place, we have a clean floor. We have clean tables to eat off of. They are not like your trestle tables and benches. Your floor of thick wooden boards was covered with dirty rushes or plants. Fleas and rats live there, and dirty dogs and pigs get to come in and sniff around. My dog Shorty gets to come in at home and sniff around under the table.
>
> Our food is soft drinks and hamburgers. Widow Daventry serves ales and wine to her customers. She sells bread for a penny. Wine costs a penny, too. My hamburger, drink, and fries cost my dad over four dollars. The widow has a big piece of meat that hangs from her kitchen ceiling and it's covered with flies. I haven't seen this at McDonald's.
>
> I enjoyed writing my letter to you. Catch you later.
>
> Your friend,
>
> Rollie Jones

4. The teacher may want to bind class letters together that come from a single unit of study like this one on *Crispin* and the Middle Ages. These can accordingly become a publication for sharing with classmates.

FURTHER READING

Allan, K. K., & Miller, M. S. (2005). *Literacy and learning in the content areas: Strategies for middle and secondary school teachers* (2nd ed.). New York: Houghton Mifflin.

Tompkins, G. E. (2005). *Language arts: Patterns of practice* (6th ed.). Upper Saddle River, NJ: Merrill/Prentice Hall.

Vacca, R. T., & Vacca, J. A. L. (2005). *Content area reading: Literacy and learning across the curriculum* (8th ed.). New York: Allyn & Bacon.

References

Allan, K. K., & Miller, M. S. (2005). *Literacy and Learning in the content areas: Strategies for middle and secondary school teachers* (2nd ed.). New York: Houghton Mifflin.

Baker, R. (1977). The effects of informational organizers on learning and retention, content knowledge, and term relationships in ninth grade social studies. In H. L. Herber & R. T. Vacca (Eds.), *Research in reading in the content areas: Third report* (pp. 148–149). Syracuse, NY: Syracuse University Reading and Language Arts Center.

Billmeyer, R., & Barton, M. L. (2002). *Teaching reading in the content areas: If not me, then who?* (2nd ed.). Aurora, CO: Mid-continent Research for Education and Learning.

Brozo, W. G., & Simpson, M. L. (1999). *Teachers, readers, learners: Expanding literacy across the content areas* (3rd ed.). Upper Saddle River, NJ: Prentice Hall.

Carmine, D., Silbert, S., Kame'enui, E. J., Tarver, S. G., & Jungjohann, K. (2006). *Teaching struggling and at-risk readers: A direct instruction approach.* Columbus, OH: Merrill/Prentice Hall.

Combs, M. (2006). *Readers and writers in primary grades: A balanced and integrated approach, K–4* (3rd ed.). Upper Saddle River, NJ: Merrill/Prentice Hall.

Cooper, J. D. (2000). *Literacy: Helping children construct meaning* (4th ed.). Boston: Houghton Mifflin.

Cooter, R. B., Jr., & Flynt, E. S. (1996). *Teaching reading in the content areas: Developing content literacy for all students.* Englewood Cliffs, NJ: Prentice Hall.

Cunningham, P. (2000). *Phonics they use* (3rd ed.). New York: Longman.

Cunningham, P., & Allington, R. (1994). *Classrooms that work.* New York: HarperCollins.

Cunningham, P. M., Moore, S. A., Cunningham, J. W., & Moore, D. W. (1995). *Reading and writing in elementary classrooms: Strategies and observations* (3rd ed.). White Plains, NY: Longman.

Donelson, K. L., & Nilsen, A. P. (1997). *Literature for today's young adults* (5th ed.). New York: Addison Wesley Longman.

Fernald, G. (1943). *Remedial techniques in basic school subjects.* New York: McGraw-Hill.

Frayer, D. A., Frederick, W. C., & Klausmeier, H. J. (1969). *A schema for testing the level of concept mastery.* Technical Report No. 16. Madison, WI: University of Wisconsin Research and Development Center for Cognitive Learning.

Frey, N., & Fisher, D. (2006). *Language arts workshop: Purposeful reading and writing instruction.* Columbus, OH: Pearson Prentice Hall.

Gipe, J. P. (2006). *Multiple paths to literacy: Assessment and differentiated instruction for diverse learners, K–12* (6th ed.). Upper Saddle River, NJ: Merrill/Prentice Hall.

Graves, M., Juel, C., & Graves, B. (1998). *Teaching reading in the 21st century.* Needham Heights, MA: Allyn & Bacon.

Gunning, T. (2005). *Creating literacy instruction for all students* (5th ed.). Boston: Allyn & Bacon.

Harris, A. J., & Sipay, E. R. (1990). *How to increase reading ability: A guide to developmental and remedial methods* (9th ed.). New York: Longman.

Hopkins, L. B. (1987). *Pass the poetry, please!* New York: Harper & Row.

Johns, J., & Lenski, S. D. (2001). *Improving reading: Strategies and resources* (3rd ed.). Dubuque, IA: Kendall/Hunt.

Manzo, A. V. (1969). The ReQuest procedure. *Journal of Reading, 11,* 123–126.

Norton, D. E., & Norton, S. E. (2003). *Through the eyes of a child: An introduction to children's literature* (6th ed.). Upper Saddle River, NJ: Merrill/Prentice Hall.

Norton, T., & Land, B. L. (1992). A multisensory approach to teaching spelling in remedial English. *Teaching English in the Two-Year College, 19,* 192–195.

Reutzel, D. R., & Cooter, R. (2000). *Teaching children to read: Putting the pieces together* (3rd ed.). Columbus, OH: Merrill.

Robinson, F. (1946). *Effective study.* New York: HarperCollins.

Roe, B. D., & Smith S. H. (2005). *Teaching reading in today's middle schools.* Boston: Houghton Mifflin.

Roe, B. D., Stoodt, B. D., & Burns, P. C. (2001). *Secondary school literacy instruction: The content areas* (7th ed.). Boston: Houghton Mifflin.

Ruddell, R. B., & Ruddell, M. R. (1995). *Teaching children to read and write: Becoming an influential teacher.* Boston: Allyn & Bacon.

Sampson, M. B., Rasinski, T. V., & Sampson, M. (2003). *Total literacy: Reading, writing, and learning* (3rd ed.). Belmont, CA: Wadsworth/Thomson.

Strickland, D. S., Galda, L., & Cullinan, B. E. (2004). *Language arts: Teaching and learning.* Belmont, CA: Wadsworth/Thomson Learning.

Taylor, B., Harris, L. A., Pearson, P. D., & Garcia, G. (1995). *Reading difficulties: Instruction and assessment* (2nd ed.). New York: McGraw-Hill.

Tempke, C., Martinez, M., Yokota, J., & Naylor, A. (2002). *Children's books in children's hands: An introduction to their literature* (2nd ed.) Boston: Allyn & Bacon.

Tierney, R. J., & Readence, J. E. (2000). *Reading strategies and practices: A compendium* (5th ed.). Boston: Allyn & Bacon.

Tompkins, G. E. (2005). *Language arts: Patterns of practice* (6th ed.). Upper Saddle River, NJ: Merrill/Prentice Hall.

Tompkins, G. E. (2006). *Literacy for the 21st century: A balanced approach* (4th ed.). Upper Saddle River, NJ: Merrill/Prentice Hall.

Vacca, J. A. L., Vacca, R. T., & Gove, M. K. (2000). *Reading and learning to read* (4th ed.). New York: Addison Wesley Longman.

Vacca, R. T., & Vacca, J. A. L. (2005). *Content area reading: Literacy and learning across the curriculum* (8th ed.) Boston: Pearson. Allyn & Bacon.

Wood, K. D., & Dickinson, T. S. (Eds.). (2000). *Promoting literacy in grades 4–9: A handbook for teachers and administrators.* Boston: Allyn & Bacon.

Children's Literature and Textbook References

Allard, Harry, and James Marshall. *Miss Nelson Has a Field Day*. Houghton Mifflin, 1985.

Avi. *Crispin: The Cross of Lead*. New York: Hyperion, 2002.

Baron, Harold, Solomon C. Steinfeld, and Robert A. Schultheis. *Practical Record Keeping and Bookkeeping*. South-Western Thompson Learning, 1988.

Bass, Herbert J. *Our Country*: *People in Time and Place*. Silver Burdett Ginn, 1993.

Bender, Lionel. *Lizards and Dragons*. Children's Press, 1991.

Bernstein, Vivian. *American Government*: *Freedom, Rights, Responsibilities*. Steck-Vaughn, 1996.

Bolt, Robert. *A Man For All Seasons*. Random House, 1962.

Brenner, Martha. *Abe Lincoln's Hat*. Illustrated by Donald Cook. Random House, 1994.

Brown, Marc. *Arthur's Teacher Trouble*. Brown, 1994.

Buffett, Jimmy, and Savannah Jane Buffett. *The Jolly Mon*. Illustrated by Lambert Davis. Harcourt, 1988.

Chapman, Cheryl. *Pass the Fritters, Critters*. Illustrated by Susan L. Roth. Four Winds, 1993.

Cherry, Lynne. *A River Ran Wild*. Harcourt, 1992.

Christopher, Matt. *The Dog that Called the Signals*. Illustrated by Bill Ogden. Brown, 1982.

Climo, Shirley. *The Egyptian Cinderella*. Illustrated by Ruth Heller. HarperCollins, 1989.

Cooney, Timothy and others. *Scott Foresman Science*. Addison-Wesley Educational Publishers, 2000.

Cooper, Elizabeth K. and others. *HBJ Science*. Orlando, FL: Harcourt Brace Jovanovich, 1989.

Dahl, Roald. *Charlie and the Chocolate Factory*. Knopf, 1964.

Frankel, Alona. *Prudence's Book of Food*. HarperCollins, 2000.

Gardiner, John Reynolds. *Stone Fox*. Crowell, 1980.

Garraty, John A. *The Story of America*. Holt, 1991.

George, Jean Craighead. *How to Talk to Your Dog*. HarperCollins, 2000.

Giff, Patricia Reilly. *Next Year I'll Be Special*. Illustrated by Marylin Hafner. Dutton, 1980.

Glubok, Shirley. *The Art of Ancient Egypt Under the Pharaohs*. Atheneum, 1968.

Goble, Paul. *The Girl Who Loved Wild Horses*. Bradbury, 1978.

Golenbock, Peter. *Teammates*. Illustrated by Paul Bacon. Harcourt, 1990.

Hopkins, Lee Bennett, ed. *Ring Out Wild Bells*: *Poems about Holidays and Seasons*. Illustrated by Karen Baumann. Harcourt, 1992.

Horne, Paul, Jr. *South Carolina: Its History and Geography*. Atlanta & Clairmont, 2006.

Hubbard, Guy. *Art in Action*. Harcourt, 1996.

Jackson, Ellen. *Cinder Edna*. Illustrated by Kevin O'Malley. Lothrop, Lee, & Shepard, 1994.

Jacobs, Joseph. *English Fairy Tales, 1898*. Illustrated by John D. Batten. Dover, 1967.

Kent, Jack. *The Blah*. Parents Magazine, 1970.

Lasky, Kathryn. *The Librarian Who Measured the Earth*. Little, Brown, 1994.

Lauber, Patricia. *The News about Dinosaurs*. Simon & Schuster, 1989.

Leaf, Munro. *The Story of Ferdinand*. Illustrated by Robert Lawson. Viking, 1936.

Leodhas, Sorche Nic. *Gaelic Ghosts*. Illustrated by Nonny Hogrogian. Holt, 1964.

Lionni, Leo. *Fish Is Fish*. Pantheon, 1970.

Lloyd, Alan, et al. *Gregg Keyboarding and Personal Applications*. McGraw-Hill, 1987.

Martin, Rafe. *The Rough-Face Girl*. Illustrated by David Shannon. Putnam's, 1992.

Mayer, Mercer. *Just Me and My Dad*. Golden Books, 1995.

Numeroff, Laura. *If You Give a Mouse a Cookie*. Illustrated by Felicia Bond. Harper, 1985.

Palanti, Margerie. *Piggie Pie*. Illustrated by Howard Fine. Clarion, 1998.

Parish, Peggy. *Dinosaur Time*. Illustrated by Arnold Lobel. Harper-Collins, 1974.

Parish, Peggy. *Play Ball, Amelia Bedelia*. Harper & Row, 1972.

Parks, Rosa. *I Am Rosa Parks*. Dial Books for Young Readers, 1997.

Perdomo, Willie. *Visiting Langston*. Illustrated by Bryan Collier. Holt, 2002.

Pfister, Marcus. *The Rainbow Fish*. Translated by J. Alson James. North-South Books, 1992.

Polacco, Patricia. *Pink and Say*. Philomel, 1994.

Prelutsky, Jack, ed. "The Man in the Moon As He Sails the Sky." *Poems of A. Nonny Mouse*. Illustrated by Henrik Drescher. Knopf, 1989.

Rosenberg, Liz. *Monster Mama*. Illustrated by Stephen Gammell. Putnam, 1993.

Rowan, James P. *I Can Be a Zookeeper*. Children's Press, 1985.

Rylant, Cynthia. *When I Was Young in the Mountains*. Dutton, 1982.

Schmitt, Conrad, and Protase W. Woodford. *Communicating in Spanish*. McGraw-Hill, 1991.

Seuss, Dr. *My Many Colored Days*. Illustrated by Steve Johnson and Lou Fancher. Knopf, 1996.

Sheldon, Dyan. *The Whales' Song*. Illustrated by Gary Blythe. Dial Books for Young Readers, 1991.

Slier, Debby, ed. *The Real Mother Goose Book of American Rhymes*. Illustrated by Patty McCloskey-Padgett, Bernice Loewenstein, and Nan Pollard. Scholastic, 1993.

Sutherland, Zena, and Myra Cohn Livingston, eds. *The Scott, Foresman Anthology of Children's Literature*. Scott, Foresman, 1984.

Thayer, Jane. *The Puppy Who Wanted a Boy*. Morrow, 1985.

Waddell, Martin. *Farmer Duck*. Illustrated by Helen Oxenbury. Candewick Press, 1992.

Watkins, Patricia A., and Glenn K. Leto. *Holt Life Science*. Holt, 1994.

Wiesner, David. *Free Fall*. Lothrop, 1988.

Wiesner, David. *Sector 7*. Clarion Books, 1999.

Winter, Jeanette. *Follow the Drinking Gourd*. Knopf, 1988.

Yolan, Jane. *Owl Moon*. Illustrated by John Schoenherr. Philomel, 1987.

Yolan, Jane, ed. *Jane Yolan's Mother Goose Songbook*. Musical Arrangements by Adam Stemple. Illustrated by Rosekrans Hoffman. Caroline House. 1992.